Dusty,

As you will

more a part of this book than
you may realize. Thanks for your
support, but more importantly, thanks
for your friendship! Tell Shanna & the kids
yours, "Hi."
Christ
Gal 1:10

_____

Game Changers

Understanding Effective Church Membership

Chester L. Proctor IV

WestBow
PRESS
A DIVISION OF THOMAS NELSON

WestBow Press books may be ordered through booksellers or by contacting:

WestBow Press
A Division of Thomas Nelson
1663 Liberty Drive
Bloomington, IN 47403
www.westbowpress.com
1-(866) 928-1240

Because of the dynamic nature of the Internet, any web addresses or links contained in this book may have changed since publication and may no longer be valid. The views expressed in this work are solely those of the author and do not necessarily reflect the views of the publisher, and the publisher hereby disclaims any responsibility for them.

Any people depicted in stock imagery provided by Thinkstock are models, and such images are being used for illustrative purposes only. Certain stock imagery © Thinkstock.

Scriptures taken from the Holy Bible, New International Version®, NIV®. Copyright © 1973, 1978, 1984, 2011 by Biblica, Inc.™ Used by permission of Zondervan. All rights reserved worldwide. www.zondervan.com The "NIV" and "New International Version" are trademarks registered in the United States Patent and Trademark Office by Biblica, Inc.™ All rights reserved.

ISBN: 978-1-4497-8362-4 (sc)
ISBN: 978-1-4497-8361-7 (e)
ISBN: 978-1-4497-8363-1 (hc)
Library of Congress Control Number: 2013904161

Printed in the United States of America

WestBow Press rev. date: 04/11/2013

FORWARD - KEN BEVEL

I have truly enjoyed reading *Game Changers*. Through experience, compassion, and clarity of the gospel message, Chester conveys the basic essentials of helping leaders understand the importance of "equipping the saints for the work of ministry" and helping new believers develop a relationship with Christ and His church. As a Connections Pastor, I can honestly identify with the characters and completely understand their realistic journey through life. Both Chester and I, along with many others in ministry, have come to realize "connecting" is an important step in the Christian discipleship process that should be approached prayerfully to help others understand the importance of each member working together to see unbelievers come to a loving and meaningful relationship with Jesus Christ.

Although this book focuses on developing effective church membership, the author does a great job in telling the story in a fictitious setting. The story is seen through the eyes of a couple who initially desires to find joy and fulfillment through accomplishing life goals. This scenario will look very familiar to many of us as it unravels the issues of life and the false hope they sometimes present. However, in their quest for contentment, the Lord captures their attention through a number of circumstances, which ultimately lead them both to critical decision points in their lives. Thankfully, the Lord has dispatched faithful servants to help the couple navigate through the difficult times. What an awesome picture of the Body of Christ.

By the end of this story, the Lord prompted me to re-examine my own life and commitment to the carrying the Gospel to the nations. This is of great personal benefit, because it helps me to guard against complacency. At the same time, it challenged my thoughts on going farther to ensure others are connected. Oftentimes we fail to see the impact of not "going the extra mile" to ensure others are being connected. This would be similar to delivering a very important package to a person's street instead of the home address. By our lack of not "going the extra-mile," we lose valuable time and sometimes the package. As leaders and followers of Christ, our desire should be to "go the extra-mile" to see the Body of Christ operate effectively while spreading the gospel in our homes, community, and nation.

Before the completion of this book, my prayer is that, this story will reignite a burning desire in each of us to see the Body of Christ grow through salvation, follow in obedience through baptism, and make a commitment to serve. Our aspiration will not be to sit on the sidelines each Sunday, but our desire will be to become "Game Changers" who work together to see unbelievers come to a loving and meaningful relationship with Jesus Christ.

Ken Bevel
Senior Associate Pastor
Connections and Major Events
Sherwood Baptist Church

DEDICATION

To my Wife Heather, children Andrew and Ava Grace, and Ministry Assistant Jessica Boaen, who stood by me every step of the way and helped carry the load that came along with writing this book and ministry as a whole.

To the senior citizens of my Bible study at Summer's Landing Assisted Living Facility who listened to me read every single word of the rough draft as I wrote it: Jewell Lovelace, Eleanor Robinson, and Nell Thigpen. You are very special women and thank you for "adopting" me!

In memory of Willena Miller, Merrill Ewing, Wynette Cook of Summer's Landing who went on to Glory Land before the book was finished.

ACKNOWLEDGEMENTS

As I sat down to write my acknowledgements, I grew nervous that I might leave someone out. However, at the risk of doing so, I have limited these down to the people who played a very important role in the completion of this book.

First off, it would be arrogant of me to skip over the most important influence in my life and in this book. Without God's grace and guidance it wouldn't have been possible for me to sit down and put these thoughts on paper. God's provisions, direction and encouragement through the study and preparation for this book has made it worthwhile to my spiritual growth, regardless of whether it sells a single copy.

Another strong influence has been my wife, Heather. From the moment I mentioned the idea of writing a book, Heather has encouraged me every day. Sometimes, she's encouraged me by asking, "When are you going to work on your book?" And yet other times her encouragement has been more direct, such as, "You need to work on your book today!" As I typed that, I couldn't help but smile and at the same time be thankful for her support. The countless hours I spent in front of the computer hammering away at this book, she selflessly kept the kids entertained in another room of the house. From time to time she would interrupt my progress to make sure I had a meal or to ask me how it was going. She will probably never know, this side of Heaven, how much she co-authored this book by simply doing what she does best, taking care of our family. *When God made you, He must have been thinking about me.* Thanks Honey!

When I first tossed around the idea of writing this book, I

was surprised at the number of people who laughed at the idea. In fact, I wasn't even sure if I'd take the time to sit down and actually finish it. But, a good friend of mine, Joe King, could always be counted on to send a text message or ask me at church, "How's the book coming?" And if I hadn't written anything in a week or two, he'd lovingly scold me and tell me to get back to work! Friends like that are rare, and I've had my opportunities to "scold" him in the past too, but I'm eternally thankful for his desire to see this book completed and his willingness to push me when necessary. Thanks, Joe!

To a dear former co-worker, Trina Baldwin, who listened to every idea , and then patiently listened as I fine-tuned each little detail around and changed it over and over. Your continued patience and listening skills proved to be just what was needed as I ironed out the details of the Michaels' lives. You may not have realized what a big part you were playing at the time, but I assure you a major part it was. Thanks for your support!

In the book, I mentioned Dusty Martin. Dusty was our former Youth and Children's Pastor at Tabernacle Baptist Church. Along with Joe, Dusty didn't laugh when I mentioned the idea of the book. In fact, his response was, to "go for it." Dusty wasn't with us much longer, but we've kept in touch since God moved him to Kentucky. During that time, he's always quick to ask how it's coming and make sure I'm making progress. But, most importantly, his prayers have been felt during this extensive process. Thanks Dusty!

It might be too much of a generalization to say this, but behind every good man is a great wife and behind every great pastor is a very busy ministry assistant. I wouldn't go as far as to call myself a great pastor, but my ministry assistant has been very busy this year. Without your support, graceful criticism, editing eye, and love for God and my family this book couldn't have been completed. Thank you Jessica Boaen for you unwavering support and assistance, all the way down to the words on the inside cover.

I wish to acknowledge a dear friend; one who also double checked my work for mistakes, supported me through this process and encouraged me to make a difference! A man who came to join us on staff during the final stages of the book and author as well, Kevin Shipp pointed me in the direction of a huge money saver and that was through the book *Write in Style* by Bobbie Christmas. Not only did Kevin proof *Game Changers,* but he also spent time encouraging me and answering "new author" questions, to which I had a million. Thanks Kevin!

And last but definitely not least is the last person to read and edit this manuscript before it made its way to WestBow Press. A teacher, turned colleague and finally friend. It's my honor to thank Mrs. Betty Fulton for the countless hours you selflessly gave to make sure the commas and capitalizations were in the right place. From the days you "forced" us to memorize the Prologue to the Canterbury Tales, which inspired my pilgrimage in 2000 to Canterbury Cathedral, to the time you still spend today pouring out your knowledge, inspiration and love to the next generation of leaders. Allow me to humbly say, the honor of having you edit this text was all mine. God bless and thank you very much! (Oh! Tell Mark I said Hi!!!)

And to all of you not mentioned that dropped me an encouraging email, Facebook message, text or comment. Thank you for your love, support and prayers during this process. It has been a pleasure to write this book and an honor to call each of you friends.

Blessings,

Chester

INTRODUCTION

"Why in the world did I pick up this book?" If you weren't wondering that before, you're probably wondering now after reading this first sentence. Then again, you might already know why you picked it up. Maybe this is an assigned reading for a college or seminary class. Perhaps you are on the staff at a church and your Senior Pastor has required you to study this book. Maybe you picked it up for some light reading at a conference. There are many different possibilities, but more than likely you fall into one of these two last categories. You are either a Pastor with a desire to lead your flock into becoming effective members or you are a member of a church with a desire to "do more."

Something important to keep in mind before you read this, however, is to understand that although there will be specific topics covered in the membership class section, this book is not written as a "how to." Instead, it is a guide to discovering how and why effective membership is possible and necessary, not how to implement it in your church.

As you will read in the pages that follow, there is a proper order for everything and to become a true, effective member of God's church, you must follow the order He has set in place. After all, I Corinthians 14:33 says, *"For God is not a God of disorder but of peace. As in all the congregations of the saints."* Therefore, it is safe to assume that God's order is perfect - and will bring peace.

At the time I started this book, I was the Associate Pastor of Connections at Tabernacle Baptist Church in Vidalia, Georgia. However, now that it is finished, I have transitioned to the position of Associate Pastor of Connections, Children and Small

Groups. All of these positions have allowed me to implement effective membership into our process of teaching the Gospel and making disciples. Through this book, you will meet and walk alongside Brian and Audrey as they move to town, attend church, and become effective members. Brian and Audrey are a fictitious married couple who represent a very real population of lost souls. You may not be able to identify with them right away, but by the end of their story, you will have found yourself lurking among the pages.

Examine this book with an open heart. Read the scriptures contained herein, but also study them in your Bible. Pray about each of them and most importantly, ask God to reveal these truths to you. I have prayed over each chapter, page and word. I have spent much time in prayer with this manuscript asking the Lord to make clear the necessary deletions and additions to this text. I encourage you to do the same thing when it comes to the changes you need to make in your own life to become an effective member. After all, if you believe what you are about to read and don't ask for the Lord to transform you, you've simply read another book and achieved momentary joy, but not a life-changing experience.

It is my hope and prayer that you laugh, cry and praise the Lord as you read. But most importantly, I pray that "your" God grows, and as He grows, you become finite. For only then can we begin to understand just how amazing He is.

Blessings as you read and as He changes you!

Chester

PART 1

The First Requirement
- Salvation

CHAPTER 1

A New Location

"That's it! We've finally made it to our new home." Audrey Michaels looked at her husband Brian and smiled.

"I'm not sure about this place, Brian" she said, "It's a lot smaller than Atlanta or even Statesboro, and we don't know anyone."

"Sure we do honey. We know the Robinsons, and with the size of this town, it won't be long before we know plenty of people." Brian glanced up and down the street before he looked back to his wife. He noticed her worried look and put his arm around her.

"Look," he said, "everything will be all right." Audrey forced a smile, but she wasn't sure her husband was right.

Audrey always thought her intuition was pretty good, and once her mind was made up, arguing with her was futile. After she graduated high school, Audrey moved from Atlanta to Statesboro and attended Georgia Southern University, against her parent's wishes. Both her parents graduated from the University of Georgia, and they desperately wanted their daughter to follow in their footsteps as a Bulldog. But, with her mind made up she traveled further south.

While she attended Georgia Southern, her cousin Melissa convinced Audrey to meet her boyfriend Henry and their friend Brian in Atlanta. Audrey reluctantly agreed and drove up from Statesboro to meet the trio at Phillip's Arena for an *Earth, Wind and Fire* tribute band performance, which with the exception of their rendition of *Fantasy*, disappointed all of them.

A few more dates, and only one more tribute concert, and

1

the two fell in love. After he graduated from Georgia Tech, Brian moved to Statesboro and they got married while Audrey completed her degree and began her graduate program. Although Audrey's parents loved Brian as a person, they weren't keen on the idea of their daughter marrying a Yellow Jacket. But, once again, her mind was made up and the two were wed.

Brian and Audrey had been married for almost three years before they decided to leave Statesboro and move to the small town of Coventry. The Michaels didn't have any children, although a family was in their plans; their focus had been their careers. The time to settle down had arrived, and thanks to Henry Robinson's recommendation, Brian landed the job of his dreams, and they relocated to Coventry. To their amazement, Audrey was able to secure a teaching position in the Science Department at Coventry High School. The circumstances seemed perfect, except that Audrey had vowed never to move to a town smaller than Statesboro, and her unhappiness was hurting their marriage.

Audrey bent down, picked up a box that was still on the front lawn, and carried it into the house. She looked around and thought, *"I guess I'd better make the most of this."* She began to unpack her box while Brian carried box after box of his own into the house. They didn't say much to each other, except for the occasional "What about this one?" from Brian, followed by one word answers from Audrey, "bedroom," "closet," "bathroom," and so on. This routine lasted about an hour, until Brian proudly announced to his wife that he had unloaded the last box from the moving van.

"Henry will be here soon to follow me and drop off the U-Haul truck. Melissa volunteered to stay here and help you unpack."

"That's nice of her," Audrey forced herself to answer.

Brian knew his wife wasn't happy, but as they had discussed many times, they didn't have a choice. This was the nearest place to Brian's new job with a school searching for a science teacher. He decided not to press the issue and instead carried the last box to the kitchen. While in the kitchen, he heard a knock at the door.

"Familiar faces!" Henry exclaimed as Audrey opened the door. Henry was loud, boisterous and always cheerful. For Audrey, spending too much time around Henry was a difficult challenge, especially when she wanted to feel sorry for herself, as was the case for her now. They hugged, and she invited them in as Brian entered the living room.

"You ready, Brian?" Henry asked.

"You bet! Gotta get this truck back by five or they'll charge us for another night!" He picked up the keys from the hall table, kissed Audrey on her forehead, and the two men left for the U-Haul depot while Melissa pulled up a chair to help Audrey unpack.

CHAPTER 2

Here's to you, Mr. Robinson!

"Now listen here, Melissa!" Audrey exclaimed. "I'm tired, it's been a long trip and I don't want to hear more about your mumbo jumbo!"

"I'm sorry, Cuz" she said, "it's just been so wonderful and I thought it'd be a great way for you to get to know some other people."

Audrey's anger grew, "I can get to know other people just fine without going to church, claiming to believe in something that doesn't exist and playing your little church games."

Audrey was a generally nice person, but regarding matters of the church, she was adamantly against such discussions. Her father had been close friends with a Methodist Minister in Snellville, Georgia, when she was a child. The church only had about forty in attendance every Sunday. But, as the town and area grew around it, attendance increased. Eventually, the church grew into the hundreds and, as the population rose, Audrey's dad watched the politics of a growing church destroy the excitement and drive his friend had. In fact, only two months had passed before the pastor threw up his hands and quit. Although her mother always suggested that there must have been more involved than just politics, her father was convinced that church wasn't a place where he or his family would waste their time.

"You get it honest, I guess, Audrey." Melissa responded. "Uncle Don has always been against organized religion, hasn't he?"

Audrey sat on the floor in silence. Although the tension was thick, the two cousins were used to family drama. They knew time would heal their minor argument and focused on unpacking the many boxes that still littered the living room floor.

Meanwhile, a much happier exchange was taking place as Brian and Henry drove back to the Michaels' residence at Tucker Grace Lane.

"You bet I remember that!" Henry exclaimed as the two friends shared stories from their college days. "But those days are long gone and good riddance to most of them," he finished.

"Why do you say that?" Brian questioned. "Those days were amazing; we had a blast!"

Henry looked serious, "Some of those days were amazing, Brian. But, we're blessed to be alive after some of the stunts we've pulled."

Brian returned the serious look and asked, "What's gotten into you, Henry?"

"I'll tell you what's gotten into me." But, then he paused and said, "Never mind, friend. We're having a great time. Forget I mentioned it."

Henry pulled the White Jeep Wrangler into the driveway and cut off the engine. Brian spoke up as Henry opened the door, "Wait Henry, I want you to finish what you were saying."

Henry leaned back, closed the door and turned to face his friend. "Ok Brian, but remember, you asked."

Brian nodded.

"I never thought I'd say this, but I get so much more enjoyment out of the different ministry opportunities at church."

Brian rolled his eyes, "You mean like soup kitchens and nursing home visits?"

"Well, sort of," Henry smiled. "It's like this, God created us for something special. For each person it's different, and even though we share many similar gifts, talents and adventures, it is still unique to the individual."

"I don't think I follow you."

"Ok, see if this makes sense. For years you and I have lived for the moment. We lived for the excitement that we could create. It always ended, sometimes painfully and sometimes not. But, the fulfillment we looked for never stayed with us very long. Would you agree?" Brian nodded.

Henry continued, "Now what if I told you I found something that brought continual fulfillment and even on what we might consider bad days, we are still happier and more fulfilled than ever before? Would you be interested?"

Brian looked skeptical, "Sure Henry, if such a thing existed. But, you can't tell me that going to church brings that kind of happiness."

Henry smiled, "Well, no. Just going to church doesn't necessarily bring you happiness because if you're just going to go, then you're looking for that momentary fulfillment that we searched so hard for in college."

Brian looked confused again, "But you just said you got more enjoyment out of ministry opportunities or something like that, and now you're saying going to church and doing that stuff is temporary. You're not a very good teacher."

Henry let out a big jovial laugh and said, "You left out one big piece of the pie." He smiled even bigger, "I told you God created us for something special. When we figure out what it is that he created us for, our enjoyment can truly begin."

Brian sat in silence, but from the glow of the security light above the garage door, Henry could see the concerned look on his friend's face.

"What's wrong, Brian?"

Brian, unsure of what he was about to say stuttered, "I don't even know God, much less the reason he created me. It's just never been important. It's always been about what we can do, how much money we make, where we live. And even that last part is spiraling out of control. I mean, we're here, but we're not happy."

Brian looked up as tears welled in his eyes and saw Henry's big goofy grin. "What's your deal, now?" he asked.

"Brian," Henry cautiously said," I've been praying about this conversation for years. "

CHAPTER 3

An Unwelcomed Surprise

"What do you think they're doing out there?" Melissa asked as she peered through the blinds. Audrey remained on the floor unpacking a box, and although her anger had lessened, she hadn't spoken. Melissa continued to spy on the men until the Jeep door flew open and Brian climbed out.

"Here they come, here they come!" She exclaimed as if they were about to throw a surprise party.

The door opened and in walked Brian followed by Henry. Both men looked as if they had been crying, but conversely they smiled from ear to ear.

Melissa walked over to her husband and asked, "Henry, are you okay?"

"I'm fine. Been fine. Doing even better now!" The excitement in his voice sparked Audrey's interest, so much so that she stood up and approached her husband.

She looked him directly in the eyes, "Have you been crying?"

"Yes." Replied Brian. "I have, actually. But, before you ask, it's a great thing! I just got saved!"

Melissa squealed with excitement.

Audrey gave her a strange look as if to say, "What is going on with you?" but instead turned back to her husband and simply asked, "Saved from what?"

Henry motioned to his wife and said, "Guys, we have to get home, but I'm sure we'll see you soon!"

"Thanks again, Henry!" Brian said as he shook Henry's hand and simultaneously pulled him close embracing his friend. Both men patted each other on the back, twice, as if to let everyone know that this was a *man hug* and completely appropriate. Audrey and Melissa exchanged hugs with each other and then with each other's husband, before the Robinsons departed.

Audrey looked towards the window as the headlights from the Jeep grew smaller until only the tail lights were visible. Then, she turned to her husband.

"Okay," she demanded, "now tell me what's going on!"

"Sure! I'll be glad to tell you all about it," Brian responded, as he sat down on the couch. Audrey took a seat in the recliner and listened carefully.

"Henry and I were talking about the good 'ole college days. Then he started telling me about how all the searching for fulfillment is in vain if we don't look in the right place. Before I knew it we were praying..."

"Stop right there, I've heard enough," Audrey interrupted. "I thought for sure you'd have enough sense not to listen to that ridiculous nonsense. Melissa tried that on me, but apparently I'm the only grown up around here."

"But, it's not like that, Audrey."

"No! I told you I've heard enough. I'm going to bed and you, Mr. Jesus Freak, can keep yourself planted right there on the couch."

Her harsh words tore through Brian's heart like a child ripping the paper off of a present Christmas morning. She stomped up the stairs, entered the bedroom and slammed the door.

About a mile from Tucker Grace Lane, Henry glanced over at Melissa and asked, "Do you think Audrey is happy for Brian?"

Melissa frowned and said, "I don't know, Hun. I guess we'll find out tomorrow."

CHAPTER 4

Application
The First Requirement
Salvation Explained

Well, if you're still reading, you are either interested in what's going to happen with Brian and Audrey, or, as I said in the introduction, you've been required to read this book. Either way, let's talk about what has just taken place in the lives of Brian and Audrey Michaels.

I am sure you can tell Brian and Audrey were lost souls when they moved to Coventry. The term *Lost Souls* refers to someone who isn't saved. When Audrey asked Brian what he "was saved from" his answer (if she had let him finish) would have been, "saved from hell." Scripture tells us in Romans 6:23: *"For the wages of sin is death; but the gift of God is eternal life through Jesus Christ our Lord."*

We were born sinners and as a result there is a price to pay. The price for being a sinner is that we must die. No matter what, every one of us will die (of course the exception is for those alive during the rapture). However, for everyone who will call on Jesus as Lord and Savior, there is the gift of eternal life through Christ. This refers to the time spent in eternity, not on earth. In other words, those saved will, in Christ, overcome the second death (Revelation 20:6). For those who are not saved, however, the price isn't just paid upon an earthly death. The souls of the lost are also judged as guilty and sent to Hell.

Chester L. Proctor IV

The first, and most important, requirement to be an effective member of a church is to have a true relationship with Jesus Christ. In fact, when Jesus left instructions for the individual (known as the Great Command) and instructions for the church (known as the Great Commission) he made it clear that we are to do a few specific things:

The Great Command - Matthew 22:36-40 (NIV)

[36] *"Teacher, which is the greatest commandment in the Law?"*

[37] *"Jesus replied: 'Love the Lord your God with all your heart and with all your soul and with all your mind.*[38] *This is the first and greatest commandment.* [39] *And the second is like it: 'Love your neighbor as yourself.*[40] *All the Law and the Prophets hang on these two commandments."*

Consider Henry when reading this passage. We can assume (and I can assure you) that Henry believes and has professed this belief in Jesus Christ as his Lord and Savior. He has asked Jesus to forgive him of his sins and in accordance with Romans 10:9-10 and Romans 10:13, he is saved.

Additionally, it is apparent that he at least loves Brian (his neighbor) as he should. Now, critics will point out that it is much harder to love someone who we might not "like" very much. While that is true, and can get theologically deep, on the surface we are simply instructed to do it and promised that "all things are possible through Christ" (Phil. 4:13).

As I write this, I am reminded of what it's like to be a child. When I was young, my father once told me I won't always have the time or luxury to ask him "Why?" He would lovingly say, "If you're standing in the road and I say to you, 'Get out of the road' you might not have time to ask me why you should do it."

The same can be argued when it comes to directions given to

us by our Heavenly Father. Sometimes we don't have time to ask why, we must simply obey. Later on, if it's not evident as to why, we can ask by searching His Word and through prayer.

In this case, evidence is found in the way Henry helps Brian take the truck back as well the most important piece of evidence, for this is when Henry shares his faith in Christ with Brian.

The second verse of scripture we need to examine is The Great Commission:

The Great Commission - Matthew 28:19-20 (NIV)

"Therefore go and make disciples of all nations, baptizing them in the name of the Father and of the Son and of the Holy Spirit, 20 and teaching them to obey everything I have commanded you. And surely I am with you always, to the very end of the age."

How about that? He told us what he wants us to do and put it in a simple, easy to understand process. Let's examine the first part of these directions for the church (By the way, the church is made up of believers in Christ and not four walls, an important, and many times, overlooked point).

Go and Make Disciples

That's right! He said, "GO!" In February of 2012 God moved our Youth/Children's Pastor, Rev. Dusty Martin, to serve as a Senior Pastor at a church in Kentucky. His last day he was asked to preach once more, and his final point that morning was that we are to *go*. He made a very good point that in the South we tend to tell people, "Y'all come eat at our church" and "Y'all come check out our new drama team," in an attempt to reach the lost. While these methods aren't necessarily to be

> abandoned, his point was that Jesus said we are
> to "*go*" and not just tell people to "come."

Consider Henry Robinson and how he had to *go* to Brian. He had to show his friend love (by acting as a servant), and God gave him an opportunity to share his faith. That's how this works and when you finally lead that first lost soul to a saving relationship with Christ, you'll smile (and you might even cry) just as Henry did.

So How Does That Make Me An Effective Member?

As I said before, the most important part of becoming an effective member in the church is to make sure you have a **real** relationship in which you call Jesus Christ your Lord and Savior. Without Jesus as your Lord and Savior, you can still go to church. You can even serve and teach in some churches, something that I personally believe is very dangerous. But, what you can't do is please God, earn your way into Heaven or find an everlasting fulfillment. If you don't have a relationship with Jesus your work will be in vain, fruitless and very frustrating.

So, you now know the first and very crucial step. Let's go see what's happening with Brian and Audrey. I sure hope things get better. I wouldn't want to sleep on the couch two nights in a row (Actually, I've had to....it's no fun)!

PART 2

The Second Requirement - Baptism

CHAPTER 5

Tomorrow

Saturday morning arrived and the sun had already been working overtime. With just one week before school was scheduled to start, Audrey had the weekend to unpack and get her teaching materials together before Monday, the first day of pre-planning at Coventry High School. Brian was still asleep as Audrey entered the living room, coffee mug in hand and stood behind the couch. As she sipped her coffee and lovingly looked at her sleeping husband, she couldn't help but replay the events from the night before.

She knew, even when she stormed up the stairs the night before, that she wasn't really as mad at him or her cousin as she let on. But she didn't want to have a discussion concerning faith, God, church or anything similar.

Brian snorted a little and rolled to his side.

Her thoughts went from the night before to the news she had been hiding from him for many weeks now. She had been so excited to tell him and planned to inform him the night before, but with the stress of the move and the results of the previous evening she didn't know if the right time was now.

Everything was peaceful and quiet.

She couldn't help but think, *"If everyone would just stop all this God talk, we could live our lives happily ever after."*

As she pondered these thoughts, a loud knock resonated from the front door that startled her into dropping her coffee mug, which bounced off of the back of the couch, spilled the burning liquid on Brian's back and caused him to roll off of the couch.

Pain seared through his back as he screamed and kicked like a preteen girl who had just been told the Justin Bieber concert was sold out.

"Oh dear, I'm so sorry!" Audrey exclaimed. "Coming," she announced to the unwelcomed visitor. "Hang on Brian, I'll get you a towel in a minute, but, oh goodness, the door."

Audrey's anger was completely gone now, as she tried to grab a towel from a nearby box that hadn't been unpacked and was incorrectly left in the living room instead of being delivered to the bathroom. The unwelcomed visitor knocked again just before she reached for the knob. Brian stumbled out of the room, towel in hand as Audrey opened the door.

Three teenage girls stood in the doorway. They were dressed in shorts and T-shirts and two of them smiled from ear to ear.

"Hi! You must be Mrs. Michaels," the tallest of the three girls announced. "I'm Emily and this is my sister Jenny," she pointed to the blonde in the middle.

"And I'm Marie," said the third girl. "Not a sister, just a friend," she added.

Emily continued, "We all attend Coventry High. Marie and I are going to be seniors and Jenny here is a junior."

Jenny agreed with a slight nod.

"We heard you were the new science teacher and we wanted to come by and say hello."

Audrey forced a smile and said, "Well hello girls. You're right." She looked at Emily, "I'm Audrey Michaels. My husband, Brian is in the other room a little preoccupied at the moment." She smiled, for the first time in a while, a genuine smile.

"So, do you three typically show up at the new teacher's house a week before school and introduce yourselves?" She said with a chuckle.

"Oh no, Mrs. Michaels!" answered Emily. "We live across the street and Marie lives down the block. We saw the moving truck yesterday, but decided to wait until you got settled before visiting. You are settled aren't you?"

Audrey smiled again, "Not completely, but it's no problem. I'm glad you stopped by. I have some unpacking to do this weekend, but Monday morning I will be at the school setting up my classroom. I could really use some help, if you girls are interested. I'll even buy you lunch for your troubles!"

"Sure!" Emily said. "We'll be there at nine!"

Audrey thanked the students and closed the door. She turned and was startled to see Brian as he stood in the living room, with a smile of his own.

"What are you smiling at?" Audrey flirted.

"Just the most beautiful woman in the world," he flirted back. "I hope you aren't still...."

"Forgotten. Now, let's run to McDonald's and get some breakfast. We have a lot of unpacking left to do."

CHAPTER 6

What's Next?

Brian glanced at the microwave clock and saw that it was 3:56 P.M., as he entered the kitchen to answer his cell phone which vibrated across the counter.

"Hey man," he answered. The caller spoke, but Audrey couldn't make out what was being said.

"Yeah sure, that will be fine. Just text me the address and I'll be there around five. Tell him I've been unpacking all day, so I won't be dressed up or anything."

The caller responded and Brian laughed.

"Okay man, thanks!" Brian hung up the phone, looked at his wife and answered the question on her face.

"It was Henry. He wants me to come by and meet," he paused; "Um," he continued after a moment, "a friend of his."

Audrey looked distrusting, "Who is this *friend?*" She inquired.

Brian wasn't sure how he should answer this, but after unsuccessfully trying to skirt around the truth, he finally blurted out, "Pastor James, his Pastor, okay?"

Audrey looked at him seriously for a moment and then responded, "It's your life."

At a quarter before five, Brian kissed his wife, grabbed his keys and left for Henry's house. He got into his blue Dodge Dakota, plugged the address into his GPS and started down Tucker Grace Lane.

"In 500 feet, turn left on Crooked Pine Drive," his GPS

announced. A few left turns, two right turns and one wrong turn, which his GPS faithfully recalculated giving an alternate route for him to take. He pulled into the Robinson's driveway.

As he pulled up, the front door to the Robinson's house flew open, and there stood Melissa frantically waving him in. He got out of the truck and started toward the door when Melissa began to speak.

"Hey man. Good to see you alive! I wasn't sure how my cousin would react last night." She met him in the yard and gave him a hug as he responded,

"Well, it wasn't a bad night, although the couch was a little rough on my back," he chortled.

Melissa frowned, "I'm so sorry," she offered, "is this meeting tonight a bad idea?"

"No," Brian quickly stated, "it's fine. She'll be fine. I'm looking forward to meeting your pastor. I have a million questions I'm eager to ask."

"Well then," Melissa beamed again, "Let's go on in, shall we?"

Melissa showed Brian into the house and pointed down the hall, "They are in the study, first door on the left. Help yourself, I'll be in with some refreshments in a minute. Will a Coke be okay?" She asked. Brian countered with a request for a Diet Mountain Dew, which Melissa said would be doable, and he made his way to the study.

At the entrance to the study, Brian knocked and upon being invited in, opened the door. As the door opened, the two waiting men rose to their feet. Henry beamed as always, and wore a Georgia Tech T-shirt with the words "Ramblin' Wreck" across the middle. To his left was a portly gentleman, probably in his early sixties, slightly bald with salt and pepper colored hair. Brian assumed this was the pastor, and his assumption was confirmed almost instantly.

"Hello there, my boy!" The pastor spoke gently to Brian as

he extended his hand. "I'm James Hutchens, Senior Pastor of Coventry Community Church. It's a pleasure to meet you."

Brian shook hands with Pastor James and stumbled through his greeting, "Thank you sir. It's a pleasure to meet you too, Mr., er, Reverend Hutcheson."

Henry turned red with embarrassment and whispered, "It's Hutchens, Brian. Not Hutcheson!"

Pastor James laughed and said to Henry, "Don't worry about that, Deacon. I'll just hold the lad down a little longer when I baptize him!" They both let out a loud roar of laughter, but Brian only managed a forced guffaw. His laugh was the kind a person forces when he doesn't get a joke and wants to conceal it from everyone else, which is exactly how Brian felt. When the two noticed this, they laughed even harder.

As the two red-faced men laughed, the door to the study swung open and in walked Melissa with a Diet Mt. Dew in one hand and a Diet Coke in the other. She handed the Diet Mt. Dew to Brian, the Diet Coke to Pastor James and turned to Henry.

"Are you two picking on Brian?" She demanded, but the men only laughed harder.

"It's fine," Brian offered. *It wasn't even that funny,* he thought to himself.

Melissa turned to Henry and said, "Now Henry, don't spend all night poking fun at Brian, I believe you boys have some serious business to attend to." And with that, she turned around towards the door, shot a wink at Brian and left the room.

The two comedians, as Brian would later refer to them when he recalled the story to Audrey, regained their composure and took a seat as Brian followed suit.

Pastor James began to speak, "Brian. All jokes aside, Henry tells me you've made a very important decision concerning Jesus Christ. Will you tell me about it?"

Over the next thirty minutes Henry and Pastor James listened, sometimes they stopped to ask questions or laugh at something they thought would end up in a Late Night Monologue one day, as Brian shared the story about his decision to ask Jesus to forgive him for his sins and become his Lord and Savior.

After he listened to Brian's testimony, Pastor James smiled and leaned back in his chair. "Well then, it sounds as if God has really begun a work in you. Congratulations! I'm proud to call you a brother-in-Christ!"

Brian thanked him and then asked the question that had primarily been the reason for this meeting. "What next?"

"Well, let me ask you a few questions," Pastor James began. "Do you want to please God?"

Brian nodded.

"And do you want to do what He says?"

Again, Brian nodded.

"Then you must follow the order He set up for us. We call that obedience and in order for you to be obedient to His commands, you are to be baptized."

Brian looked interested, nodded, but didn't speak.

Pastor James continued, "The Great Commission tells us to go and make disciples. Disciple means student of Christ, and that process began when you gave your life over to the Lord. Then, it goes on to say, we must baptize these disciples in the name of the Father, the Son and the Holy Spirit. With me so far?" He asked.

"Yes sir," Brian answered.

"Then my son, that is what's next."

CHAPTER 7

Application
The Second Requirement
Baptism Explained

We've already learned that the first requirement for effective membership is a relationship with Christ. Now, we've learned that the next step for Brian, and anyone in his situation, is baptism by immersion. When it comes to immersion (or getting dunked, as I've heard it jokingly referred to) we are simply following the example that Christ gave us to follow. We get this from the time when John the Baptist baptized Jesus and it was then that scripture indicates Jesus was under water.

Matthew 3:16 reads;

"As soon as Jesus was baptized, he went up out of the water. At that moment heaven was opened, and he saw the Spirit of God descending like a dove and alighting on him."

The second reason we baptize by immersion deals with the original language used to describe the baptism. The Greek word that is used to describe baptism in the New Testament is *batizo* which translates as "to submerge in water."

Furthermore, baptism is the first step in obedience to Christ following salvation. Multiple times in the Bible, people are seen being saved and immediately after salvation they are baptized.

Acts 2:41:

"Those who accepted his message were baptized, and about three thousand were added to their number that day."

But, my favorite story of baptism is found in Acts 8:26 - 38 (NIV):

26 *"Now an angel of the Lord said to Philip, "Go south to the road—the desert road—that goes down from Jerusalem to Gaza." 27 So he started out, and on his way he met an Ethiopian eunuch, an important official in charge of all the treasury of the Kandake (which means "Queen of the Ethiopians"). This man had gone to Jerusalem to worship, 28 and on his way home was sitting in his chariot reading the Book of Isaiah the prophet. 29 The Spirit told Philip, "Go to that chariot and stay near it."*

30 *"Then Philip ran up to the chariot and heard the man reading Isaiah the prophet. "Do you understand what you are reading?" Philip asked."*

31 *"How can I," he said, "unless someone explains it to me?" So he invited Philip to come up and sit with him."*

32 *"This is the passage of Scripture the eunuch was reading:"*

"He was led like a sheep to the slaughter,
and as a lamb before its shearer is silent,
so he did not open his mouth.
33 *In his humiliation he was deprived of justice.*
Who can speak of his descendants?
For his life was taken from the earth."

34 *"The eunuch asked Philip, "Tell me, please, who is the prophet talking about, himself or someone*

else?" *35* *Then Philip began with that very passage of Scripture and told him the good news about Jesus."*

36 *"As they traveled along the road, they came to some water and the eunuch said, "Look, here is water. What can stand in the way of my being baptized?"*

See note below about verse 3₇

38 *"And he gave orders to stop the chariot. Then both Philip and the eunuch went down into the water and Philip baptized him."*

37Note: The NIV has a footnote that says: "Some manuscripts include here Philip said, "If you believe with all your heart, you may." The eunuch answered, "I believe that Jesus Christ is the Son of God." (italic emphasis added)

How amazing is that! I don't know about you, but I love that story. The eunuch was hungry for the word. As he studied it, he had a chance to hear about Jesus. He hears and instead of waiting on the "right day" or a "better time," he's ready to be baptized and has it done immediately. God placed Philip in the eunuch's path, to explain the Gospel to him so the eunuch could truly receive the redemptive gift of salvation.

I want to tell you a story of something that is actually taking place in my life as I write this chapter. About six months ago, a young couple named Eric and Aundrea started attending Tabernacle Baptist Church. As the Associate Pastor of Connections, I made an appointment to meet them at their house and welcome them after their second visit. At the house, we talked about Salvation, and they assured me they were both saved. I explained, as did Pastor James, that the next step was baptism. They weren't ready and as is always the case, I encouraged but never forced. Instead,

I invited them to continue to worship with us, come to some Sunday school classes and evening courses that we offer.

At the end of church last Wednesday, I was informed that they were looking for me. I scoured the church trying to find them and finally located them behind closed doors with the Senior Pastor. I hung around outside with some of the youth and our Youth Pastor until they finished. As they left the building on the way to their car, Eric came up to me and we started talking. Aundrea joined us a few minutes later.

I was elated when they informed me that they were ready to be baptized, had met with the Pastor, and he told them to schedule it with me so it could be done. They will be baptized in two weeks, and I can't wait to celebrate with them and the body of Christ their public profession and "next step*!" (Update: At the completion of this book, they were in fact baptized and are currently effective members of the church. Praise God!)*

You might be asking, "What was the point of all that?" The answer is, if you're like Brian and you've been saved but not baptized, it's time to be baptized. Make it your priority as it is the next step ordered by the Lord. On the other hand, if you're witnessing to someone, and they aren't quite comfortable about being baptized (fear of large groups, lack of understanding, etc.), be patient and pray with them. Encourage them, don't push them. Love them, don't judge them. After all, God's the one who directs our steps anyway (Proverbs 20:24).

Now, let's get back to the Michaels. We still don't know how Audrey is going to respond, and there's a baptism ceremony to attend!

CHAPTER 8

A Simple Gift

Brian wasn't keen on being baptized the next day simply because they had just moved to town and were still getting settled. Not to mention that he was afraid of how his wife would react. Regardless of her reaction, he wanted time to convince her to come with him. So, as a result, his baptism was scheduled for the next Sunday.

That night Audrey didn't ask how his meeting with Pastor James went, and Brian didn't offer to share the story. Instead, they enjoyed a nice dinner from Kentucky Fried Chicken that Brian picked up on the way home, and fell asleep watching a DVD of *I Love Lucy* reruns, a gift from Audrey's mother last Christmas.

Sunday morning, Brian couldn't shake the feeling that he should be at Coventry Community Church, but as he explained to Pastor James, he wanted to break it easy to Audrey, that he would start attending regular services next week.

For the Michaels, Sunday was usually a pretty uneventful day. But, as for this Sunday, they stayed very busy. By the evening, they had everything unpacked and sat in front of the television in their living room. The satellite provider was scheduled to meet Brian at the house sometime on Monday. He wasn't sure when the provider would arrive, because when he scheduled the appointment, the receptionist told him, "The installer will arrive sometime between 8:00 A.M. and 5:00 P.M."

Brian couldn't get over how ridiculous this seemed, but at the same time he was thankful he still had the time to get these "essentials" taken care of. After all, Brian still had another week before he was to report to the nuclear plant. In the meantime, he was forced to endure *I Love Lucy* over and over again, which he was certain had taken its toll on his sanity.

As the black and white picture flickered in the dark living room, Audrey reached for the remote and pressed pause. She turned to her husband and with a big grin on her face said, "I've got some news for you."

"Boy, do I have some news for you too," Brian thought. But, instead he simply replied, "What's that?"

"Now that we have great jobs, a nice house and a seemingly structured lifestyle, what do you want more than anything?"

Up until this weekend, his answer would have almost immediately been, "kids." But now he couldn't help but think that he would rather see his wife get saved. Although deep down his desire was her salvation, he knew better than to broach the subject at this time. So, instead, he instinctively responded, "Kids?"

Although she already wore the biggest smile Brian had ever seen, Audrey's smile grew even larger as she exclaimed, "Great! Because, we're pregnant!"

Tears began to well up in Brian's eyes as he stared through the dim light at his wife. She beamed, he beamed, and he couldn't believe the blessing that had just been placed in his life. *"A baby!"* He thought! *"What could be better than a baby?"*

CHAPTER 9

Count Your Many Blessings

"Two? Are you sure?" Audrey's voice woke Brian up out of a deep sleep.

Through his crusty sleep covered eyes, he peered at the clock on his bedside table: 8:15A.M. Monday morning had arrived and his wife prepared for her first day at Coventry High School. Although the students wouldn't return to school until the following Monday, today was her first official day as a teacher. She had eagerly anticipated this day for years. She couldn't wait to get into her classroom on the first day of pre-planning and prepare herself for the adventures of teaching high school students about biology, life sciences, and even a Chemistry class. Her dream had become a reality. That was, until the phone rang.

On the other line was her doctor from Statesboro. She was very comfortable with her OBGYN there, and, as a result, had decided to make the seventy-mile drive, one way, to and from her appointments. She was also convinced that she was better off having the baby in Statesboro, and there was nothing anyone could do to change her mind.

"Audrey," her doctor had said after they exchanged pleasantries, "I want you to brace yourself. We were examining your tests and we came across something we should have never missed. After looking at your ultrasound, we believe you have what is sometimes referred to as hidden twins. In cases like this, we miss the other baby on the ultrasound. This is rare, but can happen when we do the ultrasound as early as we did. We will be able to make a clear distinction at your twenty week visit, but again, we are pretty certain at this time that you are, in fact, having twins."

It was at this point in the conversation that Audrey's exclamation woke Brian up. Her doctor responded, "Once again, we can't be 100% sure, but we are leaning that way." Brian walked into the bathroom as Audrey hung up her cell phone.

She turned to him and said, "Well, I have some more news."

He looked at her, through sleepy eyes as if to say, *hurry up and tell me, and then leave me in here to take care of business.*

She didn't take notice of his urgency for her to excuse herself and, instead, continued on with her conversation as if he weren't even there.

"Two! The Doctor called and said we are having two! Twins! Babies, Brian. Not a baby but, babies!"

Brian remained speechless, but began to process what this meant in his mind; *Two carriers, two cribs, double the diapers, double the feedings, double the mess, double the crying . . .* After he processed this news for just a few seconds, he opened his mouth, but the only thing that came out was,

"I have to go."

Audrey was infuriated.

"Go?!" She shouted, "Go where?" "Where could you possibly be going at a time like..." and then embarrassment swept across her face. "Oh!" She said, turning a deep shade of red. "I'm sorry. I'll be downstairs."

CHAPTER 10

A Tale of Two Sisters

Promptly at 9:00 A.M., just as promised, Emily, Jenny and Marie entered Mrs. Michaels' classroom at Coventry High School. Audrey was behind her desk diligently working on a stack of papers that the principal left in each teacher's box.

"Hello ladies," she welcomed.

"Hi Mrs. M," Emily and Marie answered in unison. Jenny, just gave a wave, but remained silent.

"I have a faculty meeting at 9:15 that will probably last all morning. But, I have made a list for you." She handed it to Emily. "If you don't finish everything, that's perfectly fine. However, anything you can do will really help me. I'll be back around lunchtime and we'll talk about payment then." The girls agreed and Audrey left for her meeting.

Just before noon, Audrey walked into her room and stopped just beyond the threshold in amazement.

"Oh, wow!"

She looked around at the different posters and signs on the walls. Her bulletin board was finished, complete with the periodic table on one side and the seven ranks of biological classification on the other. The desks were in order, floors were swept, and her dry erase board had never been so clean except on the day it arrived from the factory.

"So, you're pleased?" Marie questioned with a smile.

"Yes. It's amazing."

Audrey hadn't noticed immediately, but Emily and Jenny

weren't there anymore. Marie could tell by the look on Audrey's face what she was thinking.

"They had to leave about fifteen minutes ago. Emily said they'd take a rain check on lunch. Her father called, and when he calls, they don't keep him waiting."

Audrey took a seat at her desk and looked intently at Marie. "Can I ask you a question, Marie?"

"Of course."

"I know I just met you ladies two days ago, but why is it that Jenny is so quiet? She hasn't said one word, even when I've spoken directly to her. Is everything okay?"

Marie looked down, "Well, Mrs. M, I don't really know what's going on. But I've felt weird for a long time. Emily and Jenny are step-sisters. Their parents have only been married for two years. Jenny's dad was killed in a car accident when she was little. But, Emily has tried very hard to make her feel like part of the family. As you've heard, she doesn't refer to her as a step-sister or anything."

Audrey nodded as if to say, *go on.*

"Jenny and her mother moved here when Emily and I were freshmen. Their parents got married our sophomore year, and everything seemed fine. But," she hesitated, "Jenny just never really says much. When she moved here she was in the ninth grade, so we didn't see her often. But, I do remember that when their parents got married she wasn't like this. I don't know, Mrs. M, it's hard to explain. But, something just doesn't seem right about Jenny, anymore."

Audrey could tell this conversation made Marie extremely uncomfortable, so she changed the subject.

"I am just so amazed at how great this room looks. Make sure you tell the other ladies that I am going to treat the three of you to lunch one day this week. Anywhere you want to go, name the place, and we'll go."

Marie said she would tell the others, thanked Audrey and left her with many questions and very few answers.

CHAPTER 11

I'll Take This Battle, Please.

That evening, with a satellite remote control in hand, the Michaels' settled down in bed for some good 'ole fashioned quality time with their television, a custom that swept the nation years ago, and is more than likely a common problem in marriages today. As they lay in bed the pictures moved on the screen, but neither paid attention. Instead, they each were having their own inner battle.

Audrey thought about the family across the street.

"What is going on over there? Why is this teenager from a seemingly happy environment so withdrawn?"

Audrey was taught in college that she was a mandated reporter and if she suspected any kind of abuse to a minor, she was legally required to file a report. But, she didn't know what she suspected or if she actually suspected anything at all.

"I can't go making accusations just because a teenager is withdrawn, can I? Isn't that a part of growing up? Should I talk to someone? Maybe Brian will know what to do."

Meanwhile, on the other side of their king size mattress, Brian was in a struggle of his own.

"How do I invite her to my baptism? It's in a church and she'll never go for that. But, it's six days away and I'm running out of time. If I ask her now, and she gets mad, will she reconsider before Sunday?"

Simultaneously, almost as if someone counted down from three:

3....2.....1.....Go!!!

They both turned and looked at each other.

"I need to talk to you," they said in unison.

"You go first," said Brian

"No, you."

In a comforting tone, Brian responded, "You go ahead honey, what's on your mind?"

Audrey proceeded to explain the afternoon of events and her conversation with Marie. After she was finished, the best advice Brian knew to give was to suggest that she spend some time with Emily and Jenny first. Get to know them better and perhaps even attempt to talk to Jenny one-on-one. However, Brian made his disclaimer very clear by saying,

"I'm not a teacher. I don't know what you're supposed to do in this case. So, if you suspect something is wrong, perhaps talking to your Principal is a good idea. Or even, Pastor James."

Audrey looked at him dubiously and said, "What are you getting at, Brian Michaels?"

Brian swallowed hard and said, "Look. I'm not trying to push you into going to church or anything."

"Good!"

Brian ignored the remark and continued. "But, I have made the decision to be baptized this Sunday at Coventry Community Church, and I would be very grateful if my loving, sweet, tenderhearted, wife would be there to support me."

Audrey didn't crack a smile at his feeble attempt at flattery, but after a moment of silence she said, "I'll go for you. But, don't expect this to be a weekly event in my life. If you want to go every time the doors are open, fine. As for your baptism, I'll be there. Now, I love you and I'm going to bed."

As she rolled over and turned off the light, Brian pressed the off button on the television remote. The room grew dark quickly, and as Brian drifted off to sleep, his last thoughts were, *Thanks Jesus*. Somewhere in his heart, he was almost certain that he heard the words, *you're welcome*.

CHAPTER 12

From the Parking Lot to the Door

The week flew by for Brian and Audrey and Sunday morning arrived. They were both getting ready for church when Audrey started to cry.

"What's the matter?" Brian asked, putting his hands on her shoulders.

Audrey's head was down when he approached her. She looked up at Brian.

"I've been in such turmoil over Jenny and her situation. And I don't even know if there is a situation to be concerned about!"

"Have you spoken with your principal about it yet?"

Audrey shook her head.

"Well, as I said before, you can always talk to Pastor..."

"Never mind all that!" Audrey quipped. "Speaking of Church, we'd better get going if you're going to make your baptism."

Brian knew well enough not to press the issue, so he kissed his wife on her forehead, as he was accustomed to doing when she was upset, and they finished getting ready.

Neither of them spoke until they arrived at the church. Although Brian was certain his wife's poor attitude was due to the fact that she would rather be anywhere other than Coventry Community Church at that moment, he was wrong. In fact, she wasn't very concerned about being at Church. Instead, she was consumed with thoughts of Jenny. But she didn't have to think of Jenny for long.

As they climbed the steps towards the first of three people to shake their hands before they were seated in the front row, a voice cried out to Audrey from the parking lot.

"Mrs. Michaels!"

Audrey recognized the teenage girl immediately as Emily. She turned and Emily, followed by Marie and Jenny, darted through the parking lot, up the stairs and stopped inches in front of her. Meanwhile, as he reached the front door of the church, Brian was engaged by a Church greeter with a firm handshake and welcoming smile.

Audrey politely hugged each girl as Emily invited the Michaels' to sit with them, but as she did, the greeter announced to the group, "The Michaels' have a special seat on the first row. How about you ladies join them up front, instead? " Emily nodded as the greeter opened the door and ushered them all inside.

CHAPTER 13

From the Door to the Hall

As they walked inside Brian and Audrey looked around in amazement. Audrey leaned to her husband and said, "It didn't seem this big from the outside."

Brian smiled and nodded, as he quickly returned his gaze to the building.

Although there were much bigger Churches from the area that Brian and Audrey hailed from, they hadn't visited any of them and had no idea of their size. To most, this church was small, but to the Michaels', this was simply the most impressive building they had ever been inside.

The vestibule was extremely spacious with a hall on the right side and another on the left. A sign posted in the middle of the room instructed newcomers that the Church offices were located to the right, the nursery, kitchen and restrooms were to the left and the Sanctuary was just beyond the sign, through the double doors that were propped open.

While still impressed with the first greeting they received, the Michaels' were greeted again, this time by a married couple in their early-seventies with silver hair and big smiles. The man extended his hand to Brian and spoke first.

"Welcome to Coventry Community Church, friend! I'm Sam Johnson and this is my wife Jackie." Jackie nodded and smiled.

Overwhelmed with a nervous sensation at the new experience, Brian answered.

"Hello Sam and Jackie. I'm Brian Michaels and this is my

wife Audrey." He glanced at the girls and stuttered as he tried desperately to remember their names, "and these are, Emma, Marley and Jamie."

Everyone had a good laugh, except Brian which confirmed his thoughts that he messed up at least one person's name.

Sam broke the tension, "We've known Emily and Marie since the day they were born, and Jenny has been a great addition from about, what, three years ago?" He turned to Jenny.

"Two," she quietly replied as she looked down at her feet.

This was the first time Audrey heard Jenny speak, but she wasn't surprised at the soft tone. It was shy, very timid and perfectly mimicked the teen's body language.

"Ah, yes! Two, not three." He smiled at Brian. "See Brian, no one's perfect" he said with a chuckle. Sam motioned towards the sanctuary, "In ya go. Sit where ya want."

As he spoke to Brian, Jackie looked at a paper attached to a clipboard she was holding.

"Oh wait!" She exclaimed to her husband. "His name is on the list! He's getting baptized this morning!"

Sam beamed, "Well alright, Brian!" he said as he patted him on the back. "Welcome to His family! You'll want to take these lovely ladies and sit on the front right row."

And with that, the Michaels plus three, made their way to the front row and took a seat.

CHAPTER 14

From the Hall to the Pew

Within just minutes of taking their seats, a younger man in his mid twenties walked up to Brian smiling, shook his hand first and then moved towards Audrey to greet her as well.

"Hello friend. You must be Brian." He guessed.

"Yes," replied Brian with a puzzled look on his face, which his recent greeter picked up on immediately.

"I'm sure you're wondering how I guessed your name."

Audrey replied, "I don't know about him, but I was wondering that exact thing!"

The young man laughed and said, "I'm Barry Castle, the Pastor of Student Ministries here at Coventry Community. As he said this, he gave a welcoming smile to the three girls sitting next to Audrey. "We are so glad you are here today and even more pleased to hear about your recent decision, Brian."

Brian smiled and said, "Thanks," although his nervousness grew as people poured into the sanctuary from the vestibule.

"Pastor James will be here in a few minutes," Pastor Barry continued. "He is in his study praying with the elders. As soon as he's finished, we'll begin."

Brian nodded as Pastor Barry continued, "If you need anything, just let one of our ushers know. I'd love to stay for your baptism, but I have to head out back to our Student Ministry Center." He looked at the three girls, "Are y'all staying here?"

Emily nodded, "Yes, Brother Barry, we are going to stay here with Mr. and Mrs. Michaels, if that's okay."

Pastor Barry smiled, "Of course!" He turned to Brian, "Once again, it's great to have you and your lovely wife with us this morning. God bless!" And with that, Pastor Barry made a dash from the sanctuary and disappeared into the hall.

Chapter 15

Welcome to the Main Event

Brian and Audrey sat in silence and looked around the sanctuary taking in the warmth of the members, the beauty of the interior and the sheer size of the building. As they gazed at the surroundings, loud music began and a tall skinny gentleman stepped forward with a microphone.

"Everyone, please stand as we worship our Lord this morning," he announced.

The song's lyrics, which Brian and Audrey had never heard, were displayed on two big screens which hung on either side of the sanctuary. Brian did his best to sing along as Audrey just stood motionless. She remained motionless, until she finally leaned to her husband and asked,

"This doesn't sound like church music, does it?" Brian laughed in agreement, but didn't speak.

After the music had ended, the Minister of Music instructed the congregation to have a seat and motioned for Brian to step forward. As Brian got up, Pastor James joined him, placed his arm around Brian and addressed the church.

"We are so pleased to have with us this morning our newest Brother in Christ, Brian Michaels."

The congregation erupted in applause, which startled Audrey and nearly caused her to fall out of her seat.

Pastor James continued, "Just two weeks ago, Brian here, gave his life over to our Lord and Savior, and he's ready to follow Jesus' command through the ordinance of baptism."

He turned to Brian and said, "If you will go right through that door, Brother Kevin is waiting to lead you around to the baptistery."

Brian nodded and proceeded to his right, through the door and into the hall where a middle-aged man, who Brian presumed was Kevin, waited. Kevin led him down the hall to a door with a large sign which read, "Baptistery Entrance."

Kevin spoke first, "Alright Brian, through this door is a flight of stairs leading up to the baptistery. Pastor James will meet you on the other side at the top. Are you going to be baptized in those slacks or do you have a change of clothes?"

"No, I have my bathing suit on underneath."

"Good. You can change in there and leave your clothes at the base of the stairs next to the towels we left for you."

Brian thanked Kevin as Kevin opened the door and beckoned him in. Brian entered the room and the door was closed behind him.

The small dark room at the base of the stairs was no bigger than a broom closet. A white shelf hung strategically on his left with towels and an empty space for what Brian assumed was for his clothes. He took off his coat, followed by his shirt and hung them on the door. Then after he removed his slacks, shoes and socks he started up the stairs. He could hear Pastor James say,

"I will head around to the baptistery as Brother Rob leads us in another..."

As Brian reached the top of the stairs, he saw a small pool of water in what resembled a square Jacuzzi without the jets. Four steps, with a rail on his right led down into the water. He looked up and saw Pastor James standing across from him, smiling back.

"Are you ready?" he mouthed to Brian.

Brian grew more nervous by the second, but nodded back.

As the music stopped, Pastor James stepped down into the baptistery and looked out over the choir loft down into the sanctuary.

"This is one of my favorite parts of ministry," he announced to the congregation through the microphone placed on the ledge.

As he spoke, he motioned for Brian to join him in the water. Brian took his first step into the baptistery and was surprised at how warm the water felt on his skin. He proceeded into the pool, stood next to the Pastor and looked out over the congregation.

As he gazed into the sanctuary, his heart almost stopped and his nervousness reached an all-time high. The Pastor was still speaking, but Brian wasn't listening. Instead, his eyes darted from the big screen which hung in the center of the rear part of the sanctuary and displayed a live video image of him as he stood in the baptistery, to the hundreds of people in the seats, back to the microphone that was intentionally placed on the ledge in front of him.

As he contemplated these thoughts, his silence was broken by the Pastor who said, "I have one question for you, Brian."

Brian turned slightly towards Pastor James, as the Pastor continued, "Who is your Lord and Savior?"

Brian's voice nervously cracked as he answered, "Jesus Christ."

Immediately, the sanctuary was filled with cheers of joy. Men shouted "Amen" and women exclaimed, "Hallelujah," as the congregation celebrated the proclamation of faith.

Once the celebrators quieted down, the Pastor spoke again. "My son, the fifteenth chapter of Luke, verse ten says, 'In the same way, I tell you, there is rejoicing in the presence of the angels of God over one sinner who repents.'" "Some might think it's crazy to shout and scream in the house of God, but scripture makes it very clear that the same thing happened in Heaven when you gave your life to the Lord!" As the pastor concluded his commentary, the Church began to applaud and cheer again.

Pastor James beamed a smile at Brian and placed his left hand on Brian's shoulder as he started to move around to his side.

He instructed Brian to place his own hand over his mouth and nose and spoke, "Then my brother, as instructed by our Lord and Savior in the Holy Word of God and by your public profession in Him as Lord and Savior, I baptize you in the name of the Father, the Son and the Holy Spirit."

After he finished, the pastor lowered Brian backwards into the water, submerged him completely, and then raised him back up from the pool. As Brian's head came up, he could hear the familiar sound of cheers and applause.

Pastor James smiled even bigger and embraced Brian, whispering in his ear, "Congratulations, my friend. But, this is only the beginning. It gets much more challenging from here."

Chapter 16

A Brief Discussion Application

At this point, I want to break in and give you something to consider. The last four chapters, some of which were very short, discussed key ingredients to a viable and healthy church. Those ingredients were viable, healthy and active members.

A point was made to show you, the greeter at the door of the church, the couple greeting inside of the vestibule, and the greeter (in this case, the youth pastor) who spoke to the Michaels' once they were seated. Furthermore, there was Kevin, a volunteer who was prepared to take Brian to the baptistery entrance. The volunteers who filled the baptistery, made sure it was heated, washed and dried the towels, folded them and placed them in the room at the base of the stairs.

But, that's not all! The many volunteers in the sound booth, making sure the music was ready and playing. The person running the computer that displayed the lyrics on the big screen in the front of the church and the camera operator making sure everyone could see the live video of the baptism.

Now, imagine for a second if each one of these volunteers were instead sitting in the pews waiting for someone else to step up and serve. All of these intricacies, which we tend to take for granted, are important roles that God has placed on his people.

It may not seem important to greet someone, but tell that to the person who isn't greeted and feels left out, never comes back to hear about Jesus and dies without salvation. Or it may seem unnecessary to have the video feed or a camera operator, but tell that to the person who can't see the front of the sanctuary from their seat near the back. Or, more importantly, the people who make sure the baptistery is ready for the upcoming celebration.

Despite the popular misconception, pastoral staff are in these positions *to prepare God's people for works of service, so that the body of Christ may be built up (Eph. 4:12).* Therefore, it is up to God's people (the body, believers, church) to step up and perform the works of service. If you understand this chapter, you're starting to see why we aren't just supposed to go to church, sit and then leave. God's plan for us involves so much more and it all points to the ultimate purpose of winning souls for the Kingdom.

We could probably end the book here, as far as application is concerned. However, there are those reading that may find themselves understanding and yet struggling with what their role is. Not to mention, the many unanswered questions left in the lives of Brian and Audrey. From this point on, I will leave you with more story chapters and fewer application chapters. But, remember to find yourself in these pages and then relate to the characters and we'll speak again in Chapter 27.

CHAPTER 17

When it Rains...

The rain had been falling for about an hour. Hurricane Irene pounded the Eastern coast of Florida and sent rain north across the border to Coventry. A week had passed since pre-planning began for Audrey and today was the first day of school at Coventry High.

The building and grounds were being pelted with rain, but forecasters determined that the hurricane would move further northeast than originally expected and would stay off of the coast for a few days. School officials decided that the district was far enough inland and Irene wouldn't be much more than an inconvenience, so the first day of school was to occur without fail.

Audrey grabbed her umbrella from the passenger seat and scrambled out of her car. She opened the umbrella, to shield her from Irene's wrath, and headed into the school. The 7:30 breakfast bell had just rung as she unlocked her classroom door and went in. She placed her umbrella in a stand behind her desk, pulled her chair out and took her seat.

As Audrey leaned back in her chair she spoke aloud, "Well, here you are Mrs. Michaels. Six years of education and now you're a teacher. Don't mess this up!"

She chuckled, pulled herself towards her desk and opened her grade book to the first page. In big black marker, at the top of the page, was the word, *Homeroom.*´

She had scanned over her class roster many times the

previous week, from the moment the guidance counselor placed the printout in her hands, in fact. She carefully added each child, for each respective class, to the grade book and then scanned over her entries again for accuracy's sake. She was quite proud of herself and was confident this would be a year to remember. Audrey had no clue how right she was.

CHAPTER 18

...It Pours.

The bell rang at 8:05 A.M. to inform students that they had three minutes to arrive in their homerooms. Most of the students knew where they were going, with the exception of the entire freshman class and a few new students.

Audrey stood at the door and welcomed each student as they filed into the room. Most of the students were drenched and caused a minor flood on her floor as they attempted to wring themselves out before taking their seats.

Mrs. Michaels was one of four teachers with a junior homeroom, so she wasn't surprised that she seemed more nervous than her students. They laughed, joked and picked at one another as if they were professional students without a care in the world. After what seemed to be the last student to arrive in homeroom, Audrey closed her door, walked over to her desk and picked up her grade book.

"Good morning everyone," she began. "I'm Mrs. Michaels. Please answer clearly when I call your name." The room grew somewhat quiet, although she could hear whispering and a slight chuckle from time to time.

"Ashley Adams."

"Here."

"Richard Banks."

"Here, Mrs. Michaels."

"Carson Benton."

"Here."

"Jenny Cannon." There was no response.

Audrey looked up and repeated herself,

"Jenny Cannon?" Again, nothing.

Audrey marked the space A for absent and finished calling roll. Once attendance was completed, she closed her roll book, placed it on her desk and picked up a stack of handbooks. She proceeded to pass them out while she explained to the students that a parent or guardian was required to sign the inside sheet and return it by Friday.

As she finished her instructions to the class, the public address system in her room came on.

"Mrs. Michaels?" The shrill voice of the school secretary, Martha Reynolds, addressed her.

"Yes, Ma'am?"

"Do you have Jenny Cannon this morning?"

"No ma'am, she hasn't arrived."

"Ok," Mrs. Reynolds answered back. "Thank you."

The rest of the day flew by for Audrey. She proudly passed out a syllabus to each student, explained what she expected of them and what they could expect of her, and informed her chemistry class that memorization of the Periodic Table would factor into 25% of their final grade.

At 3:15 the bell rang, and Audrey eased herself into her chair with a sigh.

"Not a bad first day!" She thought, as the principal, Roger Vickers, entered her room.

Dr. Vickers was a tall slender man who wore a pair of dark slacks, newly polished black shoes, and a white golf shirt with the school's emblem on the left breast. He spoke as he entered the room.

"So, Mrs. Michaels, how was your first day?" Audrey had been leaning back in her chair, gazing at the ceiling in deep contemplation about that very question and hadn't noticed Dr.

Vickers enter the room. His voice startled her and she quickly sat forward with a "deer in the headlights" look on her face.

"Oh goodness," she gasped. "I didn't see you there." Dr. Vickers chuckled, and then politely waited on an answer to his question. "I think it went very well. Thank you again for the opportunity."

Smiling, Dr. Vickers replied, "It's a true pleasure to have you on board. However," his face dropped, "there is something I need your help with. Can you come with me please?" He motioned for her to follow him, which she promptly did.

He led her into the hall, which to her surprise was almost completely empty of students. They walked into the main lobby, turned left and entered into a side door with a gold plated sign that read, "Teachers and Staff Only." Audrey knew this to be the rear entrance to the main office, and just inside the door, on the right was a hall that led to Dr. Vickers' office. He pushed the door to his office open and motioned her ahead of him.

Audrey walked into the office and looked around quickly. This was the first time she had been in his office, and as she entered, she noticed on the wall behind his desk hung three framed diplomas. The first, an orange and blue marked his Bachelors of Science in Social Studies Education from the University of Florida. The middle frame was gold, blue and red, and proudly displayed his Master's Degree in Educational Leadership from Western Governors University and on the far right hung the third frame which displayed his Doctorate in Education from Georgia Southern University.

His desk, Audrey noticed, was very clean and everything had its place. As she looked around, Dr. Vickers motioned for her to have a seat and he took his seat behind the mahogany desk.

"They will be here in a moment. But, before they arrive, I want to ask you a few questions."

Audrey started to grow uneasy and wondered who *they* were and what *these questions* were all about.

She nodded as Dr. Vickers continued. "How close are you to Jenny Cannon?"

Audrey's expression grew puzzled as she thought. After about ten seconds she responded, "The name sounds familiar, but I'm not sure why. Should I know her?" Dr. Vickers picked up a sheet of paper from his desk, scanned over it intently and then looked up.

"Other than the fact that she is in your homeroom, she lives across the street from you."

Audrey was still confused, although she now remembered why the name sounded familiar.

"I remember now, she was absent this morning. But, as for living across the street..." Audrey paused for a moment and realized who he was referring to. "Cannon? Is that Emily...Oh dear, I never asked their last names."

"Go on," Dr. Vickers prodded.

Audrey, thinking aloud, said; "Well, if it's Jenny from across the street then she is Emily's step-sister. They came over when we first moved in and they helped me arrange my classroom last week. We also saw them at church yesterday, but..." Audrey looked him squarely in the eyes, "What is going on here, Sir?"

Before he could answer, there was a knock at his door.

"Come in," he announced and Mrs. Reynolds opened the door.

"Dr. Vickers, Chief Mead, and Officer Roosevelt are here."

Dr. Vickers nodded and then turned his eyes back to Audrey as the two officers walked in and closed the door.

"I'm afraid," he said to her, "your questions are about to be answered."

CHAPTER 19

The Blame Game

"You have to stop blaming yourself, Audrey." Brian commanded from the entrance to their bedroom.

Audrey lay in a fetal position on their bed as she clutched her pillow and sobbed deeply into the wet mass of packaged feathers. Her sobs were so hard that she couldn't speak, and when she tried, she only cried harder.

Brian entered the room, lay down behind her and wrapped his arms around his distraught wife assuming a fetal position of his own.

"Dr. Vickers said they would let you know something as soon as there is something to tell. Until then, you can't keep beating yourself up." He pulled her closer and continued his attempt to comfort her.

"Look," he said, rolling her onto her back, "I will go make a fresh pot of coffee and you can take a nice hot shower. Then, we can sit on the couch and put in the I Love Lucy DVD. It will help take your mind off of things."

Audrey nodded as Brian wiped her matted hair from her forehead and face. Her mascara had run down her cheeks and stained their white satin sheets.

Brian helped his wife sit up on the edge of the bed and then walked into the bathroom. Audrey could hear the water from the shower as Brian fussed with the knobs to reach the desired combination of hot and cold.

He came back into the bedroom and said, "Now, go jump in

there. It will do you some good. I'll go get the coffee and DVD ready." He leaned down and kissed her forehead, before he took his leave from the room.

Audrey couldn't help but believe that she could have prevented Jenny's disappearance. She thought she had seen warning signs, and now she was convinced that she should have said something.

Audrey leaned forward and with what little energy she had left, stood up and made her way into the bathroom. With the door closed, the bathroom was filling up fast with steam and it was difficult for Audrey to see. She undressed, made her way to the shower door and stepped inside. Brian was right; the hot shower was already rejuvenating her and it was obvious to Audrey, that this was just what she needed.

Brian had just put on the pot of coffee when the doorbell rang. He glanced at the clock on the microwave, which read 8:05 P.M, before he answered the front door. He swung the door open and there stood Emily and Marie. Brian could tell the girls had been crying.

"Hi girls," he offered.

"Hi Mr. Michaels," Emily forced a response. The normal excitement and exuberance had all but vanished from the teens.

"I'm sorry to bother you at this time, but is Mrs. Michaels here?" Emily asked.

"She is, but she's in the sho...." As Brian answered, he was interrupted by a blood curdling scream from the upstairs bathroom.

He darted up the stairs, into the bedroom and threw open the bathroom door, with the girls on his heels. Audrey sat in the corner of the room on the cold tile floor; her body trembled as she gasped to catch her breath. She looked down as if to hide from the horror, with her arms wrapped around her legs and her knees pulled to her face. Brian noticed the girls behind him and quickly closed the door shutting them off from the horrific scene.

He reached into the shower, turned off the water, and then knelt down next to his wife.

"Audrey?" He spoke softly to her. "Honey, what happened?"

He placed his arm around her to comfort her, but she violently turned away and began to sob harder. Brian stood, grabbed the towel from the rack, leaned back down and wrapped the cotton shield around his wife.

"Mr. Michaels," Emily's voice came from behind the closed door. "Should I call 911?"

Brian's concerned gaze didn't leave his wife as he ignored Emily's question.

"Audrey," he continued to speak softly, "Look at me. What's going on?"

After what seemed like hours, but in reality lasted only about a minute, Audrey looked up at her husband.

Softly crying, she stammered, "The fog on the mirror, it was.... it said....*you're to blame!*"

As those accusatory words departed her lips, she buried her head in her lap and resumed the hysteria.

Brian glanced up at the bathroom mirror, but saw only a few splotchy fogged up places where the steam had settled. Puzzled, he placed his hand on her shoulder, and she didn't refuse his gesture this time. He pulled her close to his chest as he called out to Emily.

"Go ahead and call 911."

"I did Mr. Michaels. They just pulled up."

CHAPTER 20

Dx: BRP

"Brief reactive psychosis," Brian said to Henry as he and Melissa entered the waiting room at Azalea Memorial Hospital.

They both looked puzzled as Henry responded, "What is that?"

Brian handed him a brochure with a picture of a soldier and an elderly woman seated in a garden, side by side. On the top of the front cover it read, *Understanding Brief Reactive Psychosis*."

The details are all in that pamphlet," Brian offered, "but basically, the doctors are saying that she's under an enormous amount of stress with the move, the babies, and now the missing girl."

Melissa was next to speak, "But what does the missing girl have to do with Audrey?"

"Well," answered Brian, "Audrey has been worried about this girl ever since the first day she, her sister and their friend showed up at our house. Audrey was certain that she was being abused or something. I suggested she talk to her Principal, but I wasn't much help beyond that."

Henry picked up on Brian's feelings of culpability and proposed to prevent any further blame casting.

"Don't you start blaming yourself too. This isn't either of your faults. It's just, well, we don't even know what it is. What we do know is the girl is missing and the two of you aren't to blame ."

Brian nodded, but didn't speak. There was an uncomfortable

silence in the room broken moments later by Audrey's doctor who walked in and approached Brian.

"Mr. Michaels," the doctor began, "she's doing fine. We have given her something to help her sleep, and don't worry, it won't harm the babies. She will wake sometime early in the morning, but drift in and out of sleep until mid-morning tomorrow. However, I would like to talk to you about what we believe is going on."

The doctor turned his head towards the Robinsons as if to ask them to excuse themselves, but Brian interjected.

"It's okay, Doc, they're family. They can stay."

The doctor smiled, "Very well. Have a seat."

Everyone took their seat as the doctor began to explain. "I trust, by now, you've had a chance to look over the pamphlet I left?"

Brian nodded.

"Well, then, you know that BRP is a psychiatric condition that can be triggered by a very stressful event in a person's life. You mentioned to me earlier some of the stressful events that have taken place in your wife's life lately. Based on these facts, we have no reason to conclude anything except that this is a brief occurrence. Of course, we'd like to keep her here for observation and run a few more tests. Furthermore, we'd like to have her talk with our hospital psychiatrist just to make sure our diagnosis is correct. If all goes well, we can discharge her in no later than two days. "

The news brought even more despair to Brian's face.

"Of course, Doc. If that's what you think is best," he muttered.

The doctor placed his hand on Brian's shoulder and Brian looked up. "I'm sorry, Mr. Michaels. I'm sure this isn't easy, but we should have all of these questions answered very soon and hopefully you can take your wife home and go back to your lives by Wednesday afternoon or Thursday morning."

"Thanks." Brian forced a reply. The doctor nodded, stood and walked out of the waiting room as Melissa moved over to the seat next to Brian.

"Brian, let's get you home. Audrey will sleep through the night and so should you. We can all come back in the morning and be here when she wakes." Brian glanced at the clock on the wall. It was almost 2:00 am and his fatigue confirmed the late hour.

At first, Brian was resistant to the idea of leaving his wife behind, but after mounting pressure from Henry and Melissa, he begrudgingly agreed.

At 3:12 A.M. Brian had finished his shower and finally placed his head on the soft down pillow he had longed for all evening. But, although he was very tired, he couldn't go to sleep. He stared at the ceiling, only slightly visible with the assistance of the street light which streamed in through an open slit in the curtain. As he tried to rest, he couldn't help but replay the entire evening in his mind, over and over like a bad dream. No matter how hard he tried, he couldn't fall asleep. As his mind wandered, his thoughts turned to his baptism and what the pastor had said.

"It gets much more challenging from here."

"What could he have meant by that?" Brian thought. *"Did he know this would happen? No, of course not."*

Brian tossed and turned, asking these same questions followed by a highlight reel of memories. Over and over he did this until just after 4:00 A.M., when he reached over and grabbed the remote control from his bedside table and flipped the television on.

He scanned through the different channels until he reached one with a preacher who stood squarely in the center of the stage, hands in his pockets and spoke with a tone that could calm a storm with just one word.

"Satan comes to hinder the work of God in the life of the believer!" The TV preacher shouted.

"Look, look, do this. Turn in your Bibles to John 10:10 and see what the good book says!"

The Bible Brian had been gifted by the church on the day of his baptism was downstairs, but thankfully, the scripture appeared at the bottom of the screen as the preacher began to shout it from the pulpit.

"The thief cometh not, but for to steal, and to kill, and to destroy: I am come that they might have life, and that they might have it more abundantly."

The preacher looked up. "Listen here! The enemy won't stop at trying to steal, kill and destroy. But Jesus! Wooooh Jesus!" The preacher threw his hands in the air. "He died for us, not just that we would have life, but that we would have it abundantly! We are meant to live!"

With that, the congregation began to shout and holler as the preacher darted back and forth across the stage. As the commotion settled down, the man of God stopped directly in the center of the stage where Brian had witnessed the start of all the excitement, and pointed straight into the camera. Brian felt as if the preacher singled him out, personally.

"You might be asking, 'why'?" He continued, staring directly into the camera. "Why, now that I'm a Christian, do terrible things keep happening?"

Astounded, Brian sat up, and anticipated every word.

"Because, my beloved!" The preacher screamed into the microphone. "The enemy is still at work! He still has a plan!"

This wasn't the answer Brian had hoped for and he started to slump back into the bed as the preacher lowered the boom.

"But you have one who works harder! You have one who works better! You have Jesus!"

As those words entered Brian's ears, he couldn't help but shout "Amen" at the top of his lungs. Instantly, he felt silly, but at the same time rejuvenated as if he'd been sleeping for days. He flipped the television off, laid his head on his pillow, and prayed as he drifted off to sleep.

CHAPTER 21

Is it Really Better to Have Loved and Lost?

It was 6:00 A.M. when Audrey's alarm sounded, waking Brian. He reached over, shut off the alarm and picked up the phone. Next to the phone was a folded piece of paper with Coventry High School's phone number scribbled on it. Melissa had written down the number the night before and left it for Brian with instructions to call and let them know about Audrey. He dialed the number and the phone rang and rang until a voice on the other end finally answered.

"Good Morning, Coventry High may I help you?" The male voice greeted Brian.

"Yes, I need to speak with the principal please." Brian requested.

The male on the other end began to laugh, "You got him. The only one here at 6A.M. I can assure you. What can I do for you?"

Brian explained the events of the previous night to Dr. Vickers, who assured him they would take care of Audrey's classes and offered his condolences for the evening the Michaels' were forced to deal with. Brian hung up the phone, grabbed a quick shower and left for Azalea Memorial Hospital.

As he pulled into the hospital parking lot, Brian saw Henry's jeep parked nearby. He parked next to the jeep and entered the hospital, greeted by Henry and Melissa in the lobby as they patiently awaited the elevator. The three exchanged greetings as the elevator doors opened and they quickly boarded for their ride to the third floor.

The short vertical trip up two stories was filled with Brian's account of the television preacher from the night before, which brought smiles to all of their faces. Their smiles dropped quickly, however, as the doors opened and two uniformed police officers stood at the end of the hall, one of whom seemed to be in a deep discussion with the head nurse. As they exited the elevator, the nurse turned and pointed to Brian. Although they were too far away to hear her, all three of them could read her lips which said, *"That's him."*

The officers started towards Brian and met him halfway. Both were rather tall and skinny, one a blond-haired, blue-eyed woman who looked to be in her mid-twenties and the other a dark-haired, brown-eyed man who looked to be in his early forties. The female officer extended her hand first.

"Hello, Mr. Michaels, I am Officer Powell and this is Officer Hatch." The male officer smiled and picked up where the first officer left off.

"If we could have a few minutes of your time, we need to discuss something of high significance with you."

Melissa spoke up, angrily, "Listen here officers, can't this wait? This man is here to see his wife who has been..."

Officer Powell lifted her hand in a firm gesture to silence Melissa, with which she complied.

"We understand and we won't be long. But what we have to tell him takes priority. Please come with us sir."

The two officers motioned for Brian to follow them into an "on call" room, left open by the nurse they were speaking with when Brian stepped off the elevator. He walked in, and Officer Hatch closed the door behind them.

"Please, have a seat." Officer Powell offered, but Brian informed her that he would stand.

"Have it your way," she quipped. "We've asked you to step in here so we can brief you on some important developments, before you visit with your wife."

Hatch began, "I'm sure you are familiar with the missing persons report of Miss Jenny Cannon?"

Until now, Brian was unsure of Jenny's identity, but he simply nodded and Officer Powell joined in as if she had just been tagged during a tag team wrestling match.

"Well, Mr. Michaels, we understand that you and your wife were close to Miss Cannon."

"I wouldn't say we are close. She and some others helped Audrey arrange her room for school, and they live in our neighborhood. That's about it; we've only been here a few weeks."

Officer Powell frowned, "This isn't an inquisition, Mr. Michaels."

"It sure feels that way. What else do you want to know?"

Officer Hatch stepped in; "We are sorry for making you wait. We wanted you to know that we have located Miss Cannon."

Brian smiled, "Well great! Audrey will be very pleased to hear that." Officer Powell interrupted the momentary delight Brian enjoyed.

"No, what Officer Hatch means is, we've found her body." Brian's smile vanished as his knees grew weak.

"Her body?" he gasped. "You mean, she's dead?" He now realized he should have taken that seat to begin with.

Officer Hatch noticed the color in Brian's face turn from pink to white and led him to the edge of the bed. Brian sat down, looked at the ground and questioned the police officers.

"Where did you find her? How did she die?"

Officer Hatch, gently responded, "The old abandoned football field on the other side of town. That's where Miss Cannon played soccer when she first moved to Coventry. Her mother had a hunch that she might be there, apparently she went there when she was upset. We'd been by twice, but hadn't seen her. Once her mother called, we sent patrols out to the field for a more in-depth look."

Brian stared into space, but clung to every word. Officer Hatch continued, "One of our officers noticed a broken window on the visitor's press box. We cut the lock on the door and found Miss Cannon's body along with a suicide note around 7:00 A.M. this morning."

Brian looked at his watch. 9:14 am.

"Chief Mead called Dr. Vickers as soon as it was confirmed, and he informed us about your wife. He asked us to come inform you ourselves and offer our assistance in any way possible."

Brian felt ashamed. During the entire meeting with the officers, he was angry towards them. He felt as if they accused his wife of having knowledge about this disappearance. But now, he realized, they were there to help his family. He looked up at Officer Powell and then Officer Hatch.

"I'm sorry I've been rude." He offered.

Officer Powell responded, "No apology necessary, sir. We understand that you've been through a lot. And right after your baptism, your head must be spinning with questions."

Brian looked puzzled. "You know about my baptism?"

"Yup," said Powell smiling. "I was sitting right there with my husband and son, on the third row. We cheered the loudest."

This made Brian feel slightly better.

Powell offered, "If you'd like, I can make a phone call and have Pastor James come by. He won't mind, and it might do you some good."

"Yes," replied Brian. "That would be nice. Now, how am I going to tell my wife?"

CHAPTER 22

A Close Call

Pastor James arrived at 11:30 A.M. and softly knocked on the door of room 202, Azalea Memorial Hospital. He faintly heard Brian's voice invite him in through the thick pine door that separated the patients from the traffic in the hall. He pushed the door open and entered Audrey's room.

Audrey lay unconscious in her bed as Brian sat in an obviously uncomfortable hospital chair which he had pulled up next to her bedside. He stared at his wife and stroked her hand with tears in his eyes.

"Brian?" Pastor James spoke as he closed the door behind him. Brian looked up and forced a smile.

"Thanks for coming by, Pastor. I don't know what to do."

Pastor James pulled up a chair next to Brian, near the foot of Audrey's bed and leaned back, making himself comfortable as he crossed his left leg over his right knee.

The two men spoke about the tragedy of Jenny's death, and Brian told Pastor James the story from the night before. The pastor simply smiled as he witnessed Brian's countenance improve as Brian recalled how he was amazed by God. After Brian was finished, they prayed together, and Pastor James asked,

"Brian. Is there anything else you want to ask me?"

Brian nodded, "How do I tell her about Jenny?"

Pastor James' brow wrinkled as he thought for a moment before he spoke.

"Well, my boy. As hard as this might seem, it's probably best to just carefully tell her the truth."

Brian frowned at the advice as the pastor continued.

"I know what you're thinking and you're right. It won't be easy, but she's going to find out eventually. Don't you think it's best if she hears it from you?"

Again, Brian nodded as Audrey began to shift in her bed. Both men looked up at her face and she looked back, through her groggy half-opened eyes. In a hoarse voice, Audrey questioned her husband.

"Hear what from you?"

Brian squeezed her hand and lovingly replied, "We'll talk later. You need your rest."

Audrey nodded, closed her eyes and drifted off to sleep.

CHAPTER 23

The Levies Won't
Hold Forever

Two grueling days had passed since the hospital discharged Audrey and she had returned home. Brian had purposely not shared what he knew about Jenny with his wife, but he knew the time would arrive soon. Instead, he deflected all conversation as he waited on her hand and foot. Everything she needed, he took care of. Every phone call checking on her, he intercepted for fear of someone bringing up Jenny. But the time he had dreaded so much came when he least expected it.

Brian had just placed Audrey's lunch dishes in the sink, when his wife appeared in the doorway to the kitchen.

Startled he said, "What are you doing up? Go lay down, you need to rest."

Audrey showed signs of her normal self and replied, "I'm fine, but we need to talk."

Brian turned to the sink, began to wash the dishes and nonchalantly responded, "Sure, what do you have on your mind?"

"The morning I woke up at the hospital you and the pastor were in the room talking."

Brian stopped scrubbing, but didn't turn around as Audrey continued.

"He told you it would be better coming from you. What was he talking about?"

Brian set the plate down and turned off the water. He reached for a towel, dried his hands and pulled up a chair across from her at the table. They both sat in silence for about a minute before Audrey pried again.

"Brian, honey? Are you having an affair?" Brian was shocked and quickly defended himself.

"No, Audrey. I promise, it's nothing like that."

"Then what is it?"

Brian looked down, "It's about Jenny Cannon."

Audrey's expression grew from demanding to worry. "Is she okay?"

Brian looked up at his wife and reached across the table taking her hands in his. "Something terrible has happened. I'm afraid, she's dead."

Audrey's eyes welled up and her face turned red as she pulled her hands from Brian and placed them over her mouth. Brian got up from the table, grabbed his chair and placed it next to his wife. He put his arms around her and pulled her close as Audrey spoke through her hands.

"How?"

"Suicide," Brian answered. He watched as the invisible levies in front of his wife's eyes crumbled beneath the pressure of the tears they were built to withstand. Her face fell into his chest as she wrapped her arms around his body. Brian was unsure of how to proceed or what to say, so he simply remained quiet and stroked her back as she soaked the front of his shirt with her tears.

The rest of the afternoon was filled with moments of silence followed by Audrey's wailing and sobbing. It was apparent to Brian that his guilt-ridden wife couldn't take much more. So, just after three o'clock he took his place next to her on the couch as she desperately tried to regain control of her emotions.

Concerned, he looked at her and said, "I'm so sorry. I wish there was something I could do."

She looked back at her husband, her hair matted to her face. "I have one more question," she said in a forced tone.

"Anything."

"Will you call Pastor James and ask him to come over?"

Brian couldn't believe his ears. He was so surprised, in fact that he didn't respond.

"Brian?" Audrey pressured. "Will you?"

Her persistence brought him back from his thoughts and he jumped up. "Yes, yes of course. Let me go get his number."

CHAPTER 24

The Angels Will Celebrate

Within fifteen minutes of hanging up, Pastor James had arrived at the Michaels' house. Brian welcomed him in and ushered him to the living room, where Audrey was sitting in the recliner. Her feet were up, and she was covered from her waist down with a light brown blanket. Embroidered on the blanket was the date of her anniversary, April 24, 2005. As the pastor entered the living room, she reached for the handle to lower her feet, but he interrupted her plans.

"Please, Audrey, don't stand. It's good to see you." He gently took her hand as a gesture of warmth, before he took his seat on the couch.

Brian offered the pastor a drink, which he accepted and Brian hurried off to the kitchen.

"Audrey," Pastor James began, "thank you for inviting me over today. Brian says there are some things you want to talk about." Audrey nodded as Brian entered the room, handed the pastor a Diet Coke and sat down. "Well then, consider this a chance to ask anything you want."

Audrey looked up. "Did she go to Hell?"

Pastor James looked at Audrey with an expression of compassion she had never seen before. She couldn't help but feel an inexplicable peace in the room.

"That's a tough question, Audrey." Pastor James explained. "It's tough, because I can't give you a guarantee that Jenny was saved.

What I can do, is tell you what Jenny did shortly after moving to Coventry and why I believe she's in the arms of Jesus."

Audrey nodded, interested.

"Shortly after she moved here, she began attending church with us at Coventry Community Church. One day, during our Vacation Bible School, her teacher was explaining that Jesus died on the cross for our sins. After class, Jenny approached the teacher and said that she wanted to be forgiven. They prayed together and Jenny gave her life over to the Lord. This is what it means to be saved. It was probably the happiest day of her life and if it wasn't, I've never seen her happier. She couldn't wait to tell everyone what had happened. And, of course, we baptized her the following Sunday. "

Audrey interrupted, "But, then why was she so sad and quiet? That doesn't sound like the saved Christian you're describing."

Pastor James' smiled faded. "No, no it doesn't, Audrey. About a year or so after that, she changed. In fact, the changes occurred towards the end of the last school year. To my knowledge, no one knows why she became so reserved.

It's a question I've pondered many times, and many more times recently. At her funeral I mentioned that..."

"Her funeral?" Audrey interrupted again. The thought hadn't crossed her mind that the funeral had already occurred.

Brian piped in, "It was two days ago. You were coming home from the hospital. You were in no condition to attend, but I sent flowers from us."

"Yes," offered Pastor James, "I'm sure everyone understands."

Audrey wasn't pleased with this news, but she understood and apologized for her interruption.

"No problem!" Pastor James said smiling. "Jump in with your questions at anytime. Now, what was I saying?"

"You were talking about what you said at her funeral."

"Oh yes! At her funeral I made it a point to discuss how

76

sometimes what we perceive on the outside is not completely indicative of what the person is dealing with on the inside, although for Jenny, it was a little reversed."

Audrey looked puzzled and this caused the pastor to chuckle.

"I got the same reaction when I said that the other day," he continued, "What I mean is, in Jenny's case she was suffering from something private. It was obvious in the change of her demeanor that something wasn't right. However, the condition of her heart hadn't changed."

"You mean her salvation?" Brian asked.

"Precisely," the pastor answered. "I've discussed with her many times, even as recently as a few weeks before her passing, about her relationship with the Lord. When we would talk about her Bible study, devotions, and prayer life she would light up. Just like the old Jenny we used to know. It was apparent that her love for the Lord hadn't waned in the least."

Pastor James could tell that something still bothered Audrey, so he pressed the issue.

"What's on your mind?"

Audrey thought for a moment and then said, "I just don't get it. She had such joy and such happiness. How could it get sucked away like that? How could someone who was once so happy kill herself?"

Pastor James looked at Brian, "Brian," he began, "do you remember what I whispered in your ear at your baptism?"

Brian smiled, "I sure do. You said it gets much more challenging from here." The pastor nodded and looked back at Audrey.

"Audrey, when a lost soul becomes reunited with its creator, a joy that cannot be duplicated or measured is produced in that person. It's a happiness that brings tears to the eyes of some and makes others smile from ear to ear."

Audrey nodded, as she hung on every word.

"In fact, do you remember the passage I quoted at Brian's baptism?"

Audrey shook her head.

"Well, it describes the scene in Heaven when this occurs. Luke 15:10 says, *"In the same way, I tell you, there is rejoicing in the presence of the angels of God over one sinner who repents.*

Unfortunately, the church has lessened the importance of a person getting saved. For some churches, it hasn't happened in so long that it doesn't seem important anymore. It's more important to keep the lights on, pay the preacher or keep *Mr. Moneybags* and *Mrs. Beenhereforever* happy. In other churches, it has happened so much, that the excitement has diminished because it has become part of the normal operations. Both of these views are tragic, but regardless of how man reacts, Heaven erupts in celebration."

"But," he continued, "the battle is not over. Even though that person has experienced a true conversion and will one day live in Heaven with our Lord and Savior, they still live on this earth. This earth, as I'm sure you know, is a terribly fallen and destructive place to live."

Audrey and Brian both nodded, but remained silent and listened intently.

"But, in the second part of John sixteen, verse thirty-three, Jesus gives us a promise. He says, 'In this world you will have trouble. But, take heart! I have overcome the world.'"

Pastor James took his last swallow from his Diet Coke and placed the empty can back on the coffee table. He leaned back into the chair and watched as the Gospel began to sink into Audrey's heart.

After a few moments of silence, Audrey answered her own question.

"So, what you're saying is, we don't know if a person is saved, except by what they say and do. But, you believe that she was and if she was in fact a Christian, even though she killed herself, she's in Heaven?"

Pastor James smiled and replied. "There are a lot of different views and arguments about suicide, but yes Audrey, the only sin we will not be forgiven for is rejecting Christ as our Lord and Savior. You see, if we reject the only one who has the ability to save us from our sins and ultimately Hell, then we have no reason to believe our sentence will be anything else but guilty.

There are no perfect Christians, and while being saved isn't a license to sin, it doesn't mandate that we be perfect either. The change that Jesus makes in us will give us a desire to please him through everything we do. But, it doesn't mean we will do it perfectly or even right the first time. Christ died for us, because we couldn't be perfect. Not so that we would believe in him and become perfect."

Audrey looked at Pastor James and humbly replied, "Well then, there is only one thing left to do."

"What's that?" Brian asked his wife.

"I want to be saved."

CHAPTER 25

Hold On to the Lap Bar

"I'm so excited for you," whispered Melissa.

They sat in the front row of Coventry Community Church. Two weeks had passed since her decision to be forgiven and this was the day of her baptism. Brian sat on the other side of his wife, her hand trembling in his. Just the night before, she confessed to him that she was terrified to stand in front of everyone or that she might say the wrong thing. He jokingly explained that all she had to do was publically confess Jesus as her Lord and Savior. If she could say his name into the microphone, she'd be fine.

Brian leaned over to her, "You're going to be okay. This is such a great day, I love you so much!"

Audrey gave a nervous smile, although a little forced due to her nerves, as the Minister of Music encouraged everyone to stand. At the conclusion of the first worship song, Pastor James stepped forward and as he did with Brian, motioned for Audrey to step forward and join him. She nervously stood and walked over to the pastor as he began to speak.

"What a tremendous day this will be!" He announced as he put his arm around Audrey. "Just two weeks ago, I was honored and humbled to sit in this woman's living room and witness the Holy Spirit do His work!"

The congregation began to applaud as Audrey's mind started to wander. As the pastor continued the story of her conversion, she realized she had not seen Emily in over two weeks. Audrey hadn't returned to school yet, in fact tomorrow was her first day back and only second day on the job.

The last time she had seen Emily had been in this very church at Brian's baptism. The three of them sat in the front row, right next to her. This time, the pew was occupied by Brian, Melissa and Henry. She was in such deep thought that she almost didn't hear the pastor say, "if you will go right through that door, Kevin is waiting to lead you around to the baptistery."

As Audrey disappeared into the hall, she heard the music start back up and the congregation resume worship. Just as her husband had done before her, she changed in the room at the bottom of the stairs and then made her way up to the baptistery entrance. When she reached the top, she saw Pastor James standing across from her, smiling broadly. As the music stopped, he stepped into the baptistery and motioned for her to do the same.

Audrey wondered what the view must have looked like from up there, during Brian's baptism, but at this point she was so terrified she wasn't interested. As the Pastor continued to address the congregation, another realization came to her mind and that was just how serious an emotional rollercoaster this was.

She was afraid of being in front of everyone, sad over the loss of Jenny, excited to know she had a personal relationship with Jesus and curious as to where Emily and Marie had been and how they were doing.

As she thought about these things, her concentration was broken by what sounded like chuckling in the congregation. She had been so busy thinking that she didn't hear the pastor address her. She turned to him and noticed that he wore the same goofy grin he had earlier.

"Are you ready?"

Red faced, she nodded.

"Who is your Lord and Savior?"

"Jesus Christ."

As he continued to speak, she placed her hand over her nose

and mouth and he lowered her into the water. Moments later, he raised her out of the water to the sounds of the roaring and applauding congregation. She couldn't help but smile as she hugged Pastor James and then looked out over the church. To her surprise, she saw two new additions to the front row. There stood Emily and Marie clapping away.

PART 3

The Third Requirement
- Commitment

CHAPTER 26

Obedience

"I am so sorry I missed her funeral," declared Audrey.

"Don't be sorry, we completely understand. I'm just glad you're okay." Emily reassured her.

They were seated at *Me llamo Emilio*, the local Mexican restaurant with Brian, Marie and the Robinsons.

"You two do know what the next step is, don't you?" Melissa asked. Both Brian and Audrey shook their heads. This was all new to them, and they didn't have a clue.

"It's time you become Game Changers," she told them.

Simultaneously, they both responded, "What's a Game Changer?"

Melissa turned to Henry and said, "Honey, God gave you this vision, you explain it." Henry swallowed his food, wiped his mouth with his napkin and placed it on his plate.

"First, before I explain this, I want you to understand two things. Number one; there isn't any pressure to do this. You don't need to jump into it until you are ready and have prayed about it."

The Michaels' nodded.

"The second thing you need to understand is that this is not something to take lightly. It must be taken seriously and you need to be fully committed, otherwise you are wasting your time, the time of the church, and most importantly, you won't be obedient to God."

Again they nodded and then Brian spoke. "Okay, so what is it?"

Henry waved at the waiter and indicated that he wanted a refill before he responded.

"Let me answer that by asking you a question. What does it mean to be a member of a Church?"

Brian shrugged. "I don't know. Audrey probably knows better."

Audrey frowned, "I'm not sure either. Everything I heard about Church growing up was negative. I guess being a member means you go there regularly and make it official."

"Oh, and the name of that Church appears in your obituary!" Brian added without thinking.

An uncomfortable silence crept over the table until Emily looked up from her quesadilla and said, "Oh, no worries. It's okay. Please continue."

Henry, in an attempt to redirect the conversation away from the sensitive direction it seemed to be going, continued by saying, "That's what most church members think. They believe once they are saved and baptized, they are to just sit and learn."

Brian looked puzzled, "But I still don't understand the whole Game Changer thing."

Audrey chimed in, "I do. It's like this; people get saved, baptized and then want to join the church. They are excited and can't wait to see what's next. But, when the emotional honeymoon of being saved and in a new place wears off, they become stagnant." She looked at Henry, "Am I close so far?"

"Sounds good to me," he replied.

Audrey continued, "By becoming a member, or Game Changer, at Coventry you agree to be more than just a seat warmer."

Brian looked over towards Henry, "And I suppose the Church has a plan for this?"

Henry nodded, "Yes, but as I said before, it takes prayer and commitment to become a Game Changer. This isn't something you invest an hour into and boom, you're done. It takes months and even after you finish, you never *really* finish."

Henry sipped his drink and then offered, "But hey, if you are seriously interested in knowing more, the Game Changer Orientation class is the first Tuesday night of each month at 6:00 P.M. at the church. Our Associate Pastor, Brother Reggie Johnson teaches the class. You'll like him; he's down to earth and easy to talk to."

Brian added, "You know, everyone at Church seems to be that way." Henry smiled, "That's because we're Game Changers."

CHAPTER 27

Application
Becoming a Game Changer

Well congratulations! You've discovered why the name of this book is "Game Changers." A lot has taken place since our last application chapter, and some very important developments in the lives of Brian and Audrey. This chapter will be one of the shortest, but I wanted to jump in to explain what's coming.

In the subsequent chapters, we will watch all that is involved in becoming a Game Changer. We will examine the practices and requirements that many churches are afraid of, or unwilling to do. We won't do a lot of Church government talk, but we will see how Coventry doesn't spend time on power brokers or squeaky wheels. They have Kingdom work to do, and for those not interested in doing the Lord's work, they are politely asked to move along.

This attitude seems harsh in today's Church, where we are more worried about losing money or making people mad, but at Coventry the focus is on the Lord and His Will for HIS Church. That's the whole point of being a Game Changer.

You see, the generally accepted model for church members isn't resulting in winning souls. In fact, the apathy that has crept into today's churches is inadvertently causing (or permitting) souls to perish - for eternity. If this was a game, and of course it is much more important than that, we would desperately seek a game changer, simply someone to come in and hit a home run or throw that successful "Hail Mary" and alter the direction we are heading. Today, our churches need less members and more game changers.

CHAPTER 28

Called to Membership

"I don't know why, but I'm excited to be here tonight." Audrey beamed with happiness Brian had never seen before.

Three weeks had passed since Audrey's baptism and the highly anticipated Tuesday night Game Changer's class was about to start. The recent changes in their lives made the last three weeks exciting. Plus, Audrey was almost twelve weeks into her pregnancy and everything was going well with the twins. Brian said many times, "To see the love of God flowing in our family makes me wonder why we didn't do this sooner."

"Good evening everyone."

The greeting came from a young man, slightly overweight and in his mid thirties who had just entered the room. He had dark hair and wore a blue button up shirt with khaki pants. He carried a Bible, a notebook and some papers which he put down on the desk at the front of the room. As he did, he quickly counted the number of students in the class.

"Wonderful, another orientation with 100% attendance," he announced.

There were twelve people in the class, seven men and five women, none of which Brian or Audrey recognized.

"I'm Reggie Johnson, Pastor of Connections and Assimilation here at Coventry." Pastor Reggie passed out a welcome packet to each student.

On the top of the first page was the title, *Game Changer*

Covenant, and Audrey noticed immediately that it had a signature blank at the bottom.

Pastor Reggie continued, "We will take a look at this in a moment. But, what you need to know right off the bat is the proper order."

He took a dry erase marker from the white board and began to write on it.

Salvation

Baptism

Membership

"It is important for all of you to understand that order. If we flip these words and go from the bottom up, we see the importance. You see, we can't have membership, if we haven't been baptized and we can't be baptized if we aren't a believer in Christ! Does everyone understand?"

Everyone nodded and Pastor Reggie continued.

"Good. Now, for the next three weeks we will look at Salvation. We will discuss why it's important, the different arguments as to how it comes about in our lives, and how to share our faith with others. Keep in mind, every time we start this class, someone comes up to me and says they aren't saved. That's awesome, because if you aren't and you discover that you're willing to do so, this class has served a major purpose."

"Amen!" said a voice near the back.

Pastor Reggie smiled, "Everyone say hello to Deacon Brendan Martin. You'll be glad to know that once a year, every deacon, elder and staff member goes through this class as a refresher."

A middle aged woman in the front row spoke up, "Wow, that's impressive."

Deacon Brendan chortled, "And it's required."

The class erupted in laughter at the deacon's honesty.

"But, the truth is," Deacon Brendan added, "I don't strive to be the MVP on this team, I only strive to be a game changer."

"Well said," Pastor Reggie complemented, "Now, everyone

take a look at the top sheet, it should say *Game Changer Covenant*. This sheet will serve as a guide we will use over the next four months. At the end of the course, you will be given the option to sign it or not. Those who are led to sign this will become Game Changers and those who don't," he paused for a moment and then said, "we will gladly pray for you as you seek God's Will and eventually another church."

Brian leaned over to his wife and whispered, "That seems kind of harsh." Audrey nodded as Pastor Reggie continued.

"Now, you probably think that seems kind of harsh."

Brian and Audrey looked at each other and grinned.

"But, it's like this. We love everyone! And we want everyone to come be a part of God's plan here at Coventry. But, we don't need people who aren't serious. They bog down the progress, cause dissention and become a burden on the church. Don't get me wrong, we still love them, we just don't need them."

"That's too much commitment for me," said a young man named Jake seated in the chair behind Audrey.

"It sounds like you just want to control us and I'm not interested in that."

Pastor Reggie, who was used to this because it happened in almost every orientation class, smiled and calmly responded.

"Look Jake, no one is asking you to sign anything tonight. Give us, and the Lord, four months to change your mind and heart. If at that time, you still feel this way, you can always pass on it."

Jake begrudgingly agreed to give it a chance, and Pastor Reggie continued to explain the intricacies of the course.

"Once we've completed our study on salvation, you will begin a new study on baptism. This study will also last three weeks and will be taught by Deacon Henry Robinson. Deacon Henry is actually responsible for the vision of Game Changers. By God's divine guidance, Deacon Henry compiled the schedule and curriculum for the entire course."

Audrey leaned over to her husband and whispered, "Did you know that?" Brian, who was just as surprised as she was, simply shook his head.

"Finally," Pastor Reggie continued, "the last four weeks of this course, our Associate Pastor of Student Ministry, Barry Castle, will cover the covenant. Our covenant is modeled after Pastor Rick Warren and Saddleback Church. Pastor Barry will explain how you are expected to protect the unity, share in the responsibility, serve the ministry, and support the testimony of this church.

Once you have completed the course, you will be assigned to a Game Changer, who will act as your mentor of sorts. You and your mentor will discuss what you've read in this book." He held up a copy of *The Church of Irresistible Influence* by Robert Lewis and Rob Wilkins. "Your mentor will also assist you in becoming a part of one of our small group ministries which is currently active in what Lewis calls, 'bridge building.' You have three months to read this, so don't waste any time."

"One month after you are plugged into and actively participating in a small group ministry, we will invite you to sign the covenant and be presented before the church for membership. Does anyone have any questions?"

Brian raised his hand and asked, "I don't really have a question, but I just want to point out that someone must really want to be a member here to go through all of this."

Pastor Reggie smiled and responded, "You're close Brian; they must really be called."

CHAPTER 29

A Startling Discovery

"I can't believe that it has been four months already," Audrey said with excitement.

Christmas was just two weeks away, and she was twenty-four weeks into her pregnancy. At this point the twins were developing a little more slowly than her doctor had hoped for, but otherwise the babies were healthy. The soon-to-be parents had recently found out that they would have a boy and a girl and carried on daily discussions concerning possible names, unable to agree on any of them.

"Today is going to be amazing. I can't believe we are finally becoming Game Changers at Coventry Community Church," Brian said, a smile beaming across his face.

"Brian," Audrey corrected, "we've been Game Changers for a while. That's the whole point."

Brian grinned, "I know, but today we become," he lowered his voice to a whisper and looked around as if someone was in the next room eavesdropping, "members."

They both laughed and Audrey looked at her watch. "Goodness, we've got to get going or we're going to be late for Sunday school."

Sunday school at Coventry Community Church was a little different than most. For instance, this wasn't a time where students sat around and learned about the Bible from a forty year veteran teacher, but instead this was a time for small group preparation and planning. Each community group, as they were commonly known, used this time to pray, plan and prepare their next community mission.

Sometimes, groups would use this time to actually go out into the community and serve breakfast, witness to others, and "build bridges." Brian and Audrey were in separate groups, and they liked it that way. Each one of them had his or her own gifts and were able to serve independently of each other.

For Brian's group, today was "*Serving the Servers*" and he couldn't wait. He came up with the idea for his group one Sunday after church. They were at Shoney's when he asked the waitress if she had been to church that morning. Her eyes filled with tears as she explained that she couldn't afford to take off on Sundays. She desperately wanted to attend church, but she didn't see how it was possible.

Before he left, Brian had worked out an arrangement with the manager. They agreed that once a month, Coventry Community Church would send volunteers to wait tables if the waiters and waitresses agreed to attend the early morning service at church.

Furthermore, the employees who attended church would retain their regular pay plus tips for the time worked by church volunteers. God had blessed this community group with an amazing opportunity to show these employees the love of Christ and Brian was quick to remind people that three employees gave their life to Christ as a result of being in church.

Audrey, on the other hand, continued to work through her grief over the tragic loss of Jenny Cannon and as a result, volunteered to serve with the church's crisis hotline.

Audrey answered phones and prayed with people on a regular basis, but her fulfillment truly came when she was able to serve at the hospital. Although she was content to serve through this community group, she longed for something else. Her struggle came in discovering how she could fulfill this desire.

"Hello?" Audrey picked up her cell phone. She was just about to enter the room designated for the Crisis Team.

"Mrs. Michaels, this is Dr. Vickers. I'm terribly sorry to call you so early and on a Sunday, no less."

"It's okay," Audrey reassured him, "what can I do for you?"

"I wouldn't have called if I hadn't just found out myself. You asked to be kept up to date on any developments as to why Jenny may have taken her life. Jenny's mother called me sometime on Friday, but I just checked my voicemail," Dr. Vickers stalled.

"Dr. Vickers, please. Just tell me."

"Right, sorry," he continued, "anyway, her mother was finally able to figure out the password to her Facebook account. On a hunch, she looked into the private messages and apparently there are many harassing letters sent from another student. Disgusting, vile things said to and about Jenny."

"Do you know who the student is?" Audrey inquired.

"No, apparently the student created a fake account. The message from Jenny's mother said the police are looking into it and can trace the IP address. That's all I know. I thought you'd want to know the latest."

Audrey thanked Dr. Vickers for the information and hung up. She stood outside of the room, leaned against the wall and tried to make sense of everything that Dr. Vickers had said. After a few minutes, she entered the room and began her duties as she replayed the recent conversation in her mind.

CHAPTER 30

A New Ministry

Audrey sat in her classroom as the detention bell rang on Monday of the final week before Christmas vacation. Thoughts of her excitement about she and Brian becoming Game Changers, and the words from a conversation she had with her mentor during the previous month, spun throughout her mind.

"Remember, if after you become a Game Changer you wish to start your own community group ministry, you can."

She hadn't really considered this as an option, until her conversation with Dr. Vickers the day before. As she pondered that conversation, he appeared in her doorway.

"Mrs. Michaels, I have some more news."

He entered the room and took a seat on top of one of the student's desks.

"The police located the student who sent those letters to Jenny. We had no idea this was an issue in our school, but apparently there are many students involved on both sides."

A confused expression grew across Audrey's face as she listened. "What issue are you talking about?"

Dr. Vicker's face hardened as he answered her, "Cyberbullying."

"What's that?"

"According to the alleged bully, there is a cyber gang here at Coventry High School. They have been creating social media accounts and targeting students. I'm not sure how far this goes, but the more we look into it, the darker it gets. We are going to have a mandatory staff meeting about this tomorrow afternoon. Then, the other administrators and I will be preparing over the Christmas break for next semester. I'll be honest, Audrey." He looked down, "We aren't prepared for this."

Audrey remained silent and after a short time, Dr. Vickers thanked her and left. She couldn't believe her ears. In all the countless hours earning her undergrad and postgraduate degrees, no one ever explained to her about Cyberbullying. She agreed with Dr. Vickers, at least from her point of view, they weren't prepared at all.

Audrey glanced at the clock and saw that fifteen minutes had passed since the detention bell had sounded. She grabbed her purse, locked the door, and headed straight for Coventry Community Church.

After a fifteen-minute drive, and stopping at every red traffic light from the school to the church, Audrey pulled into the parking lot and turned off the car. She walked in and greeted the secretary Joyce and then asked to see Pastor Reggie.

"Pastor Reggie," Joyce announced over the phone, "Mrs. Michaels is here to see you."

There was a slight pause and then she responded, "Right away, sir."

Joyce looked up at Audrey as she hung up the phone and said, "Pastor Reggie said you can go on down to his office; he's waiting for you."

Audrey thanked Joyce and made her way to Pastor Reggie's office. As she approached his office, the door was open and she heard him say, "Come on in."

She walked in, and as she took her seat, thanked him for agreeing to meet with her.

"Not a problem, Audrey. What's on your mind?" He inquired.

"I'm ready to start a new community group, Pastor Reggie."

Pastor Reggie smiled, but didn't respond.

Audrey continued. "It has to do with Cyberbullying. I don't know how, but I want to be involved with helping our school prepare, as well as helping victims, of this heinous crime."

Pastor Reggie leaned back in his chair, put his hands on his portly belly and rested his elbows on the arms of the chair.

"Then here's what you do," he instructed. "Pray about how you need to organize this. Then, get the information together. I need a proposal on what you wish to accomplish and how you will set out to do it. Nothing fancy, mind you, just something explaining your goals and the process you will use to achieve them. When you are ready, you will present your proposal to me and the other elders."

Audrey nodded. "I will have it for you by the start of the new year."

CHAPTER 31

A New Year, a New Set of Problems

Audrey's plan to have her ducks in a row by the start of the New Year didn't come to fruition as she had hoped. Just after Christmas, she began to experience Braxton-Hicks contractions. They were regular and her checkup in January showed that the twins were still forming at a slower rate than normal.

The holidays, plus the concern for her babies and the related stress made organizing everything much harder than she originally anticipated. But, she was determined and as she had told Pastor Reggie and Brian, her proposal would be completed and as close to perfect as she could make it, before it was presented.

The Ides of March had arrived when she was finally ready to present her ministry idea to Pastor Reggie and the elders. Fortunately, Coventry High School had already teamed up with government agencies, which included *stopbullying.gov,* and had established a strong set of policies and procedures to deal with the potential threat in the school.

Additionally, Dr. Vickers asked Audrey to head up the school's Cyberbullying Advisory Team. As part of their plan, the school's Board of Education agreed to team up with Coventry Community Church. All that was needed was the approval of the church elders.

Audrey stood in the front of the very same classroom that housed the Game Changers Orientation class. With her presentation ready to go, she addressed the men, one of whom was her dear friend and cousin's husband, Henry Robinson. In the back of the room, the elders permitted Brian to sit quietly as a sign of moral support.

After twenty minutes, Audrey was about to wrap up her presentation. She felt very confident as she noticed the different types of body language displayed by the men. Everyone present showed approval for her idea and the process in which she had proposed the implementation. She was walking the men through the final section, *Responding to Cyberbullying,* when a searing pain ripped through her abdomen. She screamed as she stumbled and clutched the wooden podium which toppled forward throwing her over the top and onto the floor.

"Audrey!" Brian yelled as he ran to her aid.

She writhed in pain and grabbed her stomach and through tears yelled, "They're coming. Owww, dear Jesus, help me!"

Two of the men called 911 from their cell phones, one jumped down on the floor with Brian, unsure of what to do to calm the situation, while the rest began to pray aloud for her and the babies. In what seemed like years to Audrey, the paramedics arrived and loaded her onto a gurney for transportation to Azalea Memorial Hospital.

"Come with me," Pastor Reggie told Brian. "We'll follow right behind them in my truck."

Pastor Reggie drove, closely following the ambulance up and down the snakelike roads until the ambulance driver could see the neon sign which read Azalea Memorial Hospital. As Brian exited the truck, he could see the paramedics as they wheeled the gurney with his entire family loaded on it, into the emergency entrance.

Brian, leaving Pastor Reggie behind, began a marathon sprint straight into the emergency entrance where he was greeted by a burly, intimidating security guard. The guard informed Brian that he would need to wait in the waiting room and as soon as there was an update, a member of the staff would come meet with him. Brian began to protest, but fortunately for him, Pastor Reggie had caught up with him and encouraged him to follow the guard's instructions.

Over the next thirty minutes, an extremely frazzled Brian had completed the piles of insurance and admission paperwork required by the hospital and eagerly anticipated an update. Henry sat next to Brian and continued to encourage him. He was in the middle of his sixth round of encouragement when a doctor walked in. She was a young woman, mid-thirties, slim, with dirty blonde hair and wore light blue hospital issued scrubs.

"Mr. Michaels?" she announced, unsure of which man was Audrey's husband.

Brian stood up. "Is she okay? Are the babies okay?"

Dr. Morris smiled and replied, "Yes, sir. Everyone is doing fine. We've got her under control, but the babies need to come out now. If you'll follow me, we'll get you dressed and you can come witness the miracle of child birth."

Brian hesitated, "But, doc, she's not due for another six weeks."

Dr. Morris turned around and took his hand.

"Yes, sir. We know. But, we don't have a choice. The babies will be very premature, but honestly, we don't have time to discuss it in detail now. For their safety, and hers, the babies have to be delivered soon."

Henry stepped up to Brian's side and placed his hand on his shoulder. "We'll be right here. Go be with your wife and kids. Remember, God's got this!"

Brian nodded and followed Dr. Morris out of the waiting room, while the men and Melissa joined hands and began to pray.

CHAPTER 32

Miracles

Close to an hour had passed when a nurse entered the waiting room and addressed the crowd.

"The twins and mother are fine, and the father, well, he will be okay too." She chuckled to herself.

The room erupted in praises to God and applause.

The nurse continued, "They are moving Mrs. Michaels to her maternity suite as we speak. You can all reconvene in the maternity waiting area and Mr. Michaels will be out to update everyone shortly, once he regains consciousness." She giggled some more and left.

Quickly, everyone gathered their belongings and made their way to the maternity waiting room. When they arrived, Brian was already waiting for them. He was amazed at the other people who had shown up while he was with Audrey. Pastor James and his wife Laura had arrived, as well as all of the wives of the Elders and Pastor Reggie's wife, Maria.

Immediately upon seeing the entourage, Brian began to cry. Melissa ran up to him and hugged him tightly.

"We are so thankful that everyone is okay!" She exclaimed through her mascara soaked eyes.

Henry handed them a box of tissues and patted his friend on the back.

"Everything is going to be okay now, my friend." Brian nodded, but still overwhelmed by the evening's events, didn't speak.

With all the commotion, Brian didn't notice Dr. Morris enter the room as well. She smiled and patiently waited for him to notice her. When he finally made eye contact, she spoke up.

"Mr. Michaels, would you like for me to update everyone?"

Brian nodded.

"Mrs. Michaels is going to be fine. She is resting now, but should be able to have a brief visit with everyone in about fifteen minutes. The twins, are definitely premature, and are currently in ICU. They will have to spend a while here, until they are fully developed and can breathe on their own. I know this seems scary, but we have every reason to believe they will both be fine in a few weeks and ready to go home.

We've been in contact with Mrs. Michaels' OBGYN in Statesboro. Her doctor had feared a possible early birth and had prescribed some medicine to help with the development of the twins' lungs. This may very well have saved their lives."

Brian began to cry again, this time out of relief, and buried his head into his hands. Melissa sat next to him and stroked his back as Dr. Morris finished her presentation.

"But, as I said before, you all have a lot to be thankful for. This whole ordeal has truly been a miracle."

Brian looked up through his teary eyes at Dr. Morris and started to thank her, but as he did, his emotions got the better of him and all he could manage was a nod.

Dr. Morris understood quite well and responded, "It was my pleasure, Mr. Michaels. Congratulations, Dad!"

Dr. Morris hadn't been gone five minutes when the same nurse from earlier walked in and announced that Brian and two guests could come and see Audrey.

Brian turned to Henry and Melissa and motioned for them to come with him. As he started out of the room, Pastor James called out to him.

"Brian, wait."

Brian spun around, "Sir?" he choked out.

"Come here, m'boy," Pastor James extended his arms and embraced Brian tightly.

"Your family has been such a blessing to us over the last eight months." Pastor James took a step back; Laura stepped in to give Brian a hug. As she did, the pastor continued to speak. "We're going to leave now and let you and your family get some rest. We'll be back tomorrow. Congrats my brother!"

Brian shook hands with the other men and women in the room as well, and thanked each one of them for their love and support. He then made his way into the maternity wing, followed by Henry and Melissa, to room 107 where Audrey was resting.

He lightly tapped on the door and heard her say *"Come in."* They entered her room and looked around.

"This is a pretty big room," Brian thought, *"especially for a hospital in such a small town."*

Brian walked over to his wife's bed, leaned down and kissed her gently on her forehead. Audrey smiled and said, "It sure has been an amazing first year in Coventry."

The other three laughed, but the looks on their faces showed more relief than humor.

Melissa and Henry sat down on the couch across from her bed, in front of the bay window that looked out into the hospital courtyard, while Brian took his place in a chair next to her bed.

"I've got some good news, Audrey." Henry reported with a smile. Audrey looked at him intently as if to say, well, get on with it.

"The elders approved your ministry idea. Once you're back on your feet, they are ready to begin."

A big smile grew across Audrey's face. "Oh, thank you so much," she exclaimed. But, almost as quickly, her smile faded.

Melissa was the one to catch this sudden change.

"Cuz? What's wrong?"

Audrey's eyes welled up as she responded. "It's just...I wish there had been a program like this before Jenny . . . you know."

Melissa nodded. "Yes, Audrey, I get it. But, remember something, God's miracles come in many forms. There's no telling how many students are better protected now, because of Jenny's tragedy."

"Yes, I know," answered Audrey as Melissa continued.

"It's hard to swallow sometimes, but Romans 8:28 promises that God will work things out for the good of those who love him. We may not fully understand, but He does and He will do what's best."

"Thanks Cuz," Audrey said. "You always know what to say."

Melissa smiled, "I do have one very important question for you." Audrey looked puzzled before she responded.

"What's that?"

Melissa's smile grew even larger.

"What are you going to name the twins?"

Through his laughter, Brian answered, "We've been struggling with that question for a while now."

Audrey was smiling again. "I haven't," she said.

They all looked at her, now intrigued.

"For our girl, Jenny, and for our boy, Cannon."

CHAPTER 33

Conclusion

I truly hope you enjoyed reading about the life of Brian and Audrey, as much as I enjoyed writing it. I believe there are so many real-life examples of how God works in our lives, beyond what makes us good church members.

Although I hope you enjoyed the fictitious story contained in this book, my greater desire is that you see what it means to be an *effective member*. It doesn't have anything to do with your age, length of time at church, the money you tithe, offerings you give or positions you hold. Being a deacon or chairman of some committee doesn't make you effective. Being a pastor or pastoral staff member doesn't make you effective. What makes you effective is that you're being used by the Creator for His Will.

Too many church members have bought into Satan's lie that if you're saved and sit in church, you're done until you die. That couldn't be more of a contradiction to what Jesus taught in the Great Commission.

At our associational children's camp each year, we sing a song by Stephen Curtis Chapman called *Live Out Loud*. In his song, he says that, "This is life we've been given, made to be lived out." The life of a Christian on earth is meant to be lived in Christ and to the fullest. We are meant to be servants to the world, not slaves mind you, but servants. We are expected, not requested, to humble ourselves before God and serve Him by ministering to the lost, hurting, suffering, desolate, needy; the list goes on and on.

I was listening to a podcast once, in which Pastor Rick Warren said, "We have to determine whether the church is here for *service* or to *serve us.*" The church member who sits on the back pew and does nothing else (okay, that's stereotypical of me, because churches are full of a lot of "do nothing" members sitting near the front) is wasting two things:

1) The space of a possible Game Changer

2) The life given to them by Christ

So, I'll leave you with this thought. If you truly want to live according to the purpose God created you for, it's time to stand up and act. Stop pretending that you're important enough in your church to simply show up and be seen. Stop buying into the lies that somehow the church is blessed to have you. There are no MVP's in the church. If you're not doing something to aid in the recovery of lost souls in your church, then the truth is, you're probably a burden and not a blessing.

Now, I know, that's a pretty harsh thing to say (we'll blame Pastor Reggie). But, I want this to be clear: God's purpose for you is ultimately going to bring Him glory. So, I ask you, is what you're doing bringing the glory to God? We need a Homerun! We need a successful "Hail Mary" pass! It's time we stop striving to be members and start working towards becoming ***Game Changers.***

CPSIA information can be obtained at www.ICGtesting.com
Printed in the USA
LVOW082335030513

332254LV00001B/55/P